MI
RECIPES
FOR ONE

Other cookery titles in the Paperfront series:

How To Boil An Egg — Simple Cookery For One
Wholefood For The Whole Family
Food Processors Properly Explained
Slow Cooking Properly Explained
Pressure Cooking Properly Explained
Deep Freeze Secrets
Basic Freezer Recipes
An Indian Housewife's Recipe Book
Right Way To Make Jams

By the same author:

Microwave Cooking Properly Explained
Out Of The Freezer Into The Microwave
The Microwave Planner — How To Adapt Your Family
    Favourites

All uniform with this book

MICROWAVE
RECIPES
FOR ONE

by

Annette Yates

PAPERFRONTS
ELLIOT RIGHT WAY BOOKS,
KINGSWOOD, SURREY, U.K.

Made and Printed in Great Britain by Robert Hartnoll Ltd., Bodmin, Cornwall.

CONTENTS

CHAPTER   PAGE

   Introduction   9
1 What Are The Advantages?   11
2 Which Microwave To Choose?   14
3 The Necessary Equipment   18
4 The Microwave's Partners   22
5 A Word About Healthy Eating   24
6 Using The Recipes   27
7 Breakfasts   32
8 Soups, Starters & Sauces   37
9 Fish   49
10 Meat & Poultry   61
11 Vegetables & Vegetable Dishes   81
12 Cheese & Eggs   95
13 Pasta & Rice & Pizzas   102
14 Desserts   111
   Index   121

ACKNOWLEDGEMENTS

The author would like to record her thanks to the following companies.

For the loan of microwave ovens for testing:
Litton, Mint House, 6 Stanley Park Road, Wallington, Surrey SM6 3EZ.
Samsung, 225 Hook Rise South, Surbiton, Surrey KT6 7LD.
Sharp Electronics, Sharp House, Thorp Road, Manchester M10 9BE.
Toshiba (UK) Ltd, Toshiba House, Frimley Road, Frimley, Camberley, Surrey GU16 5JJ.

For the loan of equipment and wrappings:
Lakeland Plastics, Alexandra Buildings, Station Precinct, Windermere, Cumbria LA23 1BQ.
Microware Information Service, 271 High Street, Berkhamsted, Herts HP4 1AA.
Terinex Ltd, Elms Industrial Estate, Bedford MK41 0ND.

This book is dedicated to my daughters, Emma and Lindsay, who always appreciate my 'work'.

INTRODUCTION

Here is my contribution to those of you who have to cook for one. I refer not only to those of you who live alone, but also to those who cook for one for any other reason. Maybe members of your family need to eat at different times? Maybe someone is on a special diet which requires food to be cooked separately? Maybe members of your household have tastes and preferences which differ greatly — maybe one of you is vegetarian? Then, of course, there are always the occasions when you are alone at a meal-time — lunch-time is a good example where I am concerned. It is this type of occasion when you (or I) may be tempted to fall into bad eating habits which in turn can result in a monotonous, unvaried diet of snacks. Taking a little time to care for *yourself* on these occasions will, I am sure, give you feelings of satisfaction and well-being.

This book aims to cut down time-consuming planning and cooking methods to a minimum — leaving you either with more time to live the rest of your busy life, or with more time in the kitchen to complete other more lengthy procedures (batch baking for the freezer perhaps?). With the help of this book, you will find cooking for one easier, more fun, and not necessarily more expensive than cooking for several.

So often I am asked for cooking times for one portion or one item. 'All the recipes seem to be geared to four people!' you complain. 'Is there a simple rule of thumb which enables me to cut the cooking time according to the quantity?' you ask. In answer to the first question, more magazines are now becoming aware of the large percentage of readers needing recipes and times for one. The answer to the second question is 'No'. There are however simple guidelines, on page 28, which will help to build up your knowledge and, more importantly, your confidence when dealing with small quantities. There are also in this book over 85 tested recipes and ideas for quick, nutritious dishes using convenient ingredients. Many of the recipes have been acquired during numerous microwave classes over the past few years. Every recipe involves *cooking* and not simply marrying two or three 'convenience' foods to make a meal. They have been written for those who are *interested* in what they eat. They are for those who are *interested* in making sure that their diet is varied, exciting, and provides the nutrients needed for a healthy lifestyle — without the slavery to the kitchen!

The subjects of defrosting and reheating are given greater emphasis in my Paperfront 'Out Of The Freezer Into The Microwave'. Similarly, 'Microwave Cooking Properly Explained' and 'The Microwave Planner' concentrate on giving information about the workings of the microwave oven and about adapting your everyday recipes.

Finally, in addition to the recipes in this book, you will no doubt have your own favourite dishes in mind. Do try them out — you won't know how good they are until you try. Doubtless you will make some mistakes (I know I do) but don't give up, learn from them, look at them as a challenge, and soon your confidence and your success rate will soar!

Annette Yates

Note: Heart Pacemakers
Microwave ovens which are well maintained are perfectly safe. However, a few *very* early types of cardiac pacemaker *may* be susceptible to interference when in close proximity to electro-magnetic fields such as those caused by microwave ovens and, incidentally, by some electric razors. If in doubt do not hesitate to seek medical advice.

1. WHAT ARE THE ADVANTAGES?

Speed
Whether you are cooking for one or for six the main advantage of microwave cooking will always be speed. In general, conventional cooking times can be cut by 60–75%. A chicken portion takes less than five minutes, a potato in its jacket takes 4–6 minutes, and a one-portion sponge pudding takes just 2 minutes — to name but a few examples.

Cost
In terms of fuel savings you cannot beat the microwave. It uses only one quarter of the power required to run a conventional oven, and cooking times are dramatically shorter. The microwave energy is directed straight into the food — none is wasted heating up the containers or the walls of the oven. Energy is used for a shorter time than in the conventional oven too — while cooking is actually taking place — plus no preheating is necessary. The lower the power level used, the less fuel is used and, finally, there is little loss of heat from the tightly-sealed unit of a microwave oven. If you are cooking for one (and previously had to heat up the conventional oven for one portion) then all these points are relevant.

Versatility

There are very few foods which cannot be defrosted, cooked or reheated in the microwave. There will always be some foods which personal taste will tell you to cook conventionally but, as you will see in the recipe pages, the possibilities are endless. Here is a brief list of items which the microwave will not cook: eggs in their shells (e.g. for making boiled egg), batter-coated foods, toast, pies, *crusty* bread and pancakes. Deep-fat frying should never be attempted in the microwave, and boiling more than 550ml/1 pt water is quicker and more economical using the electric kettle.

The microwave oven is most suitable for cooking small quantities of food, though it copes very well with large amounts when necessary too.

Food can be prepared in advance and reheated or (probably more likely when you are cooking for one) cooked as and when it is needed. Since the microwave cooks in the shortest possible time and in the minimum amount of liquid, the maximum nutritional content is retained. It is also suitable for low-fat cooking (see page 25).

Space-saving

If you are restricted to a small kitchen or area in which to prepare food, the microwave takes up a proportionally small space. This makes them very suitable for use in bedsits too. Oven sizes vary tremendously today, so there should always be a model to suit individual needs (see page 14).

Ease Of Use

A microwave oven can be plugged anywhere there is a 13 amp socket outlet. They can therefore be moved about (see page 15) when necessary. The complexity of controls varies from model to model, depending on its facilities. Once learned, however, they are simple. There are many models which incorporate just a few controls (adequate for most requirements: pages 15 and 17) so almost anyone can use them. This makes them particularly suitable for the elderly or the disabled — in fact anyone who has to look after themselves.

Clean In Use
Food can be cooked and served in the same dish, and drinks can be heated in the cup or mug. There is no direct heat to bake or burn foods on to the containers, so washing-up is cut to a minimum. Oven-cleaning is easy too. Similarly, since there is no direct heat to burn on spillages (as in a conventional oven) the oven walls are easily cleaned with a damp cloth. Finally you will find fewer cooking smells, less steam, and your kitchen/cooking area remains cool.

2. WHICH MICROWAVE TO CHOOSE?

If you have yet to purchase your first microwave oven, or if you are updating your model, you may be rather awed by the prospect that there are over 200 models from which to choose. If you are updating your present model your task will be easier since you will already be aware of any shortfalls in your existing oven. To help you whittle your choice down to just a few models, I have devised ten questions which you may like to ask yourself while looking at oven specifications. I am sure that they will also stimulate you to think of extra questions relating to your own particular needs.

1. How much space do you have and where? If you cook for one person (i.e. yourself) on a permanent basis, this is probably the first question you will ask yourself. There are several compact, suitcase-like models available which take up the minimum space on a worktop or shelf. Some types can be fixed on the wall. Check these small models carefully though if you require more than the most basic functions and wattage. Whatever size or wattage you choose, the oven will need to be positioned near a 13 amp socket outlet. All microwave ovens have vents so check where these are positioned. A surrounding area for ventilation is necessary of 5–8cm/2–3 inches.

You will also need sufficient clearance to open the door. Will you prefer a side-opening, a drop-down or an upward-opening door? Maybe you will want the oven to be built in to your kitchen — if so, check that it is suitable for this and whether there is extra cost involved.

2. How much do you want to pay? Normally this question would come top of the list, but the assumption that you will probably require a table-top version cuts down the range of prices anyway. Begin by looking in the medium price range — most cookers here should suit your basic requirements.

3. Will you want to move the oven around? Maybe you will want to move the microwave from one room to another, or perhaps outside. Maybe you will want to take it with you on self-catering holidays. These points will dictate the exterior size of the oven and its weight too. Some table-top models can be very heavy. You will notice that all ovens are heavier on one side — usually the side containing the microwave-forming valve (the magnetron).

4. How do you intend to use your oven? Look at the type of life you lead and the sort of food you eat. Will you be using your oven to cook? If so then you will probably require an oven with variable control. Are you likely to be preparing food in advance? Some models incorporate advance programming, enabling the microwaves to switch on while you are out. Some will keep your food warm on a heat-and-hold programme if you do not return home on time. On the other hand if you are likely to be doing much less cooking and more defrosting and reheating, a fairly basic machine will suit you. Look at the specifications on every model you view. Wattages vary from 400 to 700. The majority of recipes (and certainly all mine) are developed on 600–700W machines. Microwave cooking on a 400–500W machine will still be faster than conventional cooking, but if speed really is of

the essence (and we all seem to get busier by the day!) then you may become frustrated with a lower wattage. For a conversion chart if you have a lower wattage oven, see page 28. Finally, if you prepare and cook a lot of pastry or roast dishes you may like to consider a combination oven (see number 7).

5. Are you likely to be cooking for more than one person in the future? Do you entertain often? If the answer to either of these questions is 'yes' you should look at purchasing a microwave cooker with a slightly larger oven capacity than you need at present. Do not be misled by first appearances. Open the door and look at the inner cavity. Check whether it will take larger containers and larger items of food (a large chicken, a turkey, a meat joint or a large casserole, for example).

6. Do you have a grill? If not, look at those models which incorporate a browning element.

7. Are you replacing a conventional oven? Space may be limited. Perhaps you do not have a conventional oven at present and do not wish (or have the resources) to purchase two cooking appliances. There are several models of combination ovens on the market now. They are generally more expensive and larger than most microwave ovens are. They combine convection, microwave and radiant heat in the one appliance. The oven cavity is smaller than a conventional oven, making them particularly suitable for cooking for one or two.

8. Do you have the time to learn new processes? I have spoken to people who, in updating their microwave, have chosen the more complicated models. You may be told that they take the thinking out of microwave cooking — with automatic sensors doing everything bar washing the dishes! Many of these people had been perfectly happy with their former models but were now having difficulties. A common complaint was that set

programmes (some models have 25 or so) using the automatic sensor, were not cooking food to their liking. I have stressed in previous books that the degree to which food is cooked must be left to personal taste and preference. So if you are buying a microwave oven for the first time, consider carefully before buying a complicated model. This is not underestimating your intelligence, but in my experience it takes far longer to learn, and to gain confidence, in microwave cooking on a more complicated oven. Despite this, if you do have the time to get to know these machines they usually prove to be indispensable.

9. Does the colour matter? You will probably want it to fit in with your colour scheme. At the moment colours other than black, brown, beige, cream or 'wood' cost extra. Hopefully as more colour schemes are introduced, prices should come down.

10. Do you have problems in operating machines? Elderly or disabled readers will find a microwave oven a safe way to cook. There are many touch-control models available for ease of use, and for blind persons, some manufacturers can supply braille panels.

3. THE NECESSARY EQUIPMENT

Cooking Containers

Cooking containers are suitable if they allow the microwaves to pass straight through them into the food. Metal containers should not be used — the microwaves are reflected off them causing the food to take longer to cook. They could also cause damage to your oven. Plates and containers with metal decorations should not be used since the decoration will spark and blacken. Having advised against the use of metal, it *is* permissible to use small areas of smooth foil to shield delicate or thin areas of food, to prevent them from overcooking. Always follow your manufacturer's instructions carefully regarding the use of foil, never allowing it to touch the oven walls.

So what type of container is suitable? Ovenglass, glass ceramic, pottery and stoneware are suitable for cooking and will withstand high temperatures. Paper, plastic, baskets, wood, waxed paper and cardboard should be used for short-term heating only. Use kitchen paper to absorb moisture and as a cover to prevent food from spitting or splashing on the oven walls.

A vast range of containers is on offer. These have been designed specifically for the microwave — in heat-resistant plastic, glass and ceramic. Many can be used in the microwave, in the freezer and in the conventional oven too (some only up to a specified temperature). Always check with the label when you are buying equipment, to make sure it is most suitable for your day-to-day food preparation.

Checkpoints for containers
* Circular shapes are best — the microwaves can penetrate all sides of the food.

* A ring shape is excellent for larger cakes, meat loaves, etc. The slow-cooking centre, which is sometimes found when cooking in a normal circular container, is removed.

* Squares and rectangles are prone to overcooking at their corners.

* A bowl has no corners and is most suitable for foods which need stirring during cooking.

* Straight-sided containers produce better results than those with sloping sides.

Plastic Bags And Covers
Ordinary plastic bags should not be used in the microwave. It is sometimes suggested that frozen vegetables can be cooked in their original wrapping. Small amounts of vegetables microwaved for short periods may be successful, but take care that the plastic does not melt.

Microwave oven bags (and roasting bags)
These special bags are available in a range of sizes. They withstand high temperatures and are excellent for cooking single portions of fish, meat, vegetables, fruit and puddings. They are particularly useful for microwaving small quantities of soup, casseroles and for reheating plated meals. They can be used in the microwave, in the conventional oven, as a

boil-in-the-bag, and for freezer storage. When microwaving, sit the bag of food in a small, rigid container (to keep it an even, uniform shape) and remember to tie it loosely (or make a small slit in a convenient area) so that steam can escape.

Boil-in-the-bags

These are also resistant to high temperatures and are useful for single portions in the microwave, for boiling on the hob and for freezing. Some frozen foods and pre-prepared products are supplied in these bags which make them suitable for microwave cooking. Always remember to make a small slit in the bag to prevent it ballooning up (and possibly bursting) and to allow the steam to escape.

Cling film

This PVC film has proved to be the most popular covering agent over many years. Recently questions have been asked about its safety — regarding the migration of plasticisers (the component that makes it stretchy) from the film into the food during cooking. There is currently no evidence to suggest that it is harmful to our health but, until research is completed, it seems a sensible precaution if, when we use it as a cover, we avoid using it in direct contact with the food. There are alternative wrappings on the market which do not contain plasticisers. These include Purecling, Gladwrap and Saran Wrap. Remember to pierce any type of film during microwave cooking to prevent it ballooning up and to allow steam to escape.

Other Useful Accessories

* Small browning dish with a lid. Browning dishes have a special coating which reaches a high temperature when exposed to microwaves. Please note — this is the *only* type of container which should ever be put into the microwave *empty* when the oven is switched on. They are particularly useful for imitating shallow frying of meat, sausages, bacon, eggs and 'toasted' sandwiches. A browning dish with a lid will allow you to brown meat and/or vegetables before adding the remaining ingredients of a soup, sauce

or casserole and covering. Do follow the manufacturer's instructions carefully.

* Microwave rack. This is useful for two reasons. It lifts the food (particularly that which is unsuitable for stirring) off the base of the oven or turntable in order that the microwaves can gain better access to the base of the container. It can also be used to cook foods which need draining and which are best kept out of their cooking juices, e.g. bacon rashers, chicken joints.

* Small casserole with lid — preferably with straight sides.

* Kitchen paper. This is used under and on top of foods to absorb fat and moisture, and as a cover to prevent the oven walls being splashed by spitting food.

* A jug for heating liquids and for making sauces. Even though you may be cooking small quantities, the liquid must have room to rise or boil up in the jug, so choose one larger than you think necessary.

* Small bowls or ramekins for mixing very small amounts, for melting and for cooking.

* Small (550ml/1 pt) and medium (1.1 litre/2 pt) mixing bowls.

* A measuring jug, for accuracy.

* A set of measuring spoons, metric, imperial, or both.

* A small set of scales, also for accurate results.

* Wooden spoon and a small hand whisk.

4. THE MICROWAVE'S PARTNERS

When cooking for one (or for two) you will probably find that certain appliances are invaluable partners to the microwave —making food preparation more convenient, speedy and fun. Sometimes they will help you to produce better results too.

The Refrigerator
This is an obvious partner to any type of cooking appliance and ensures that we can safely buy food days in advance of cooking it. Can you imagine the time and harassment involved in shopping on a daily basis for quantities to serve one person? One point worth mentioning at this stage is that all the recipes in this book (and indeed in most other cookery books) have been tested using ingredients at room temperature. So next time a dish takes a little longer to cook, consider the margarine, the milk, the meat etc., that you have taken straight out of the refrigerator.

The Freezer (or the freezer compartment in the fridge)
As I stressed in the past, the freezer is a perfect companion to your microwave. It is no longer relegated to the 'storage

only' area but it becomes an integral part of your meal 'production line'. Food stored in the freezer is ready for immediate use. For speed and convenience, defrost frozen items in your microwave. Use your freezer to store extra portions of cooked food, cooked left-overs and everyday items such as bread rolls. Quantities of frozen vegetables, fruit, meat and fish are all assets to any microwave cook. Entire meals can then be defrosted and cooked or reheated in the microwave.

It is encouraging to note how many frozen food manufacturers are including microwave instructions on their products today. Several companies are also packaging them in microwave-suitable containers, saving us the chore of emptying food from a foil container.

The Grill
The grill is a very useful appliance — not just for making toast but for finishing off many dishes to give them a crispy brown surface. A grilled surface provides instant appeal in terms of colour, aroma and flavour. Having a grill also means that you can use it to grill items such as sausages or chops while you prepare vegetables or other items in the microwave. This can often halve the time spent in the kitchen.

The Hob
When microwaving for one the hob can come in useful for 'side-by-side' cooking. For example, cooking the spaghetti on the hob, leaving the microwave free for preparing the bolognese sauce. However it is by no means an essential partner to the microwave.

5. A WORD ABOUT HEALTHY EATING

A healthy diet is one which is balanced — giving us all the nutrients which our bodies need to live a healthy life, whether at work, at rest or at play. The variety of fresh and processed foods available, cooking methods, and often our lifestyles, can make this a particularly daunting task. Today we are continually bombarded with advice and information on achieving a healthy lifestyle. Once upon a time we were told that in order to lose weight we should cut down on starchy foods like bread and potatoes. Since then it has been realised that bread and potatoes are not the culprits. It is what we put on those bread and potatoes that makes the difference! In 1983 the NACNE* Report was published. This made five particular dietary recommendations:

1. Being overweight is associated with several health problems. Calorie intake (i.e. our source of energy) therefore should match the daily requirements for a

---

*NACNE: National Advisory Committee on Nutrition Education

person's sex, height and weight, and should be accompanied by adequate exercise.

2. Fat intake should, on average, make up 30 per cent of the total calorie intake. In the past, the majority of us ate too much. 'Saturated' fats have been linked with heart disease, so we should now eat more chicken, fish, turkey, *lean* meat, low-fat dairy products, vegetable products, and 'polyunsaturated' fats.

3. There is a link between sugar (sucrose) and tooth decay, so sugar intake should be restricted to 20kg per year.

4. Our salt intake was too high and should be cut down. Salt is naturally present in many fresh foods, and processed foods can contain a high proportion of salt. When assessing your salt intake, take these into consideration as well as the salt you may add to your plate.

5. We need fibre (it used to be called roughage) in our diet to assist the digestive tract to function properly. Fibre is found in vegetables (particularly unpeeled ones) and fruit, cereals and dried beans, peas and lentils (pulses).

Having looked at these recommendations, it is still my opinion that a balanced diet can be achieved by eating a *variety* of foods (particularly fresh foods) with *no excesses*.

Since 1983 there have been developments in food-labelling which aim to help us in our choice of foods. Not only are ingredients being listed in more detail, but the labels on many foods now also contain nutritional information and cooking instructions (including microwave cooking instructions).

So where does the microwave come into all this?

In general, the microwave oven cooks food in the least amount of liquid and in the shortest possible time. This way food retains maximum flavour, texture and dietary value.

Vitamins and flavour are not washed out into masses of cooking liquid. Flavour is therefore concentrated and so there is less need to add extra salt. Fish, meat, poultry and vegetables all cook well in the microwave. Since microwaving is essentially a moist method of cooking, it is not necessary to use fat where it may have been added in a conventional recipe, e.g. when softening vegetables for a soup, sauce or casserole. While cooking for one it can be tempting to rely on the frying pan and ready-prepared foods; now with the help of the speedy microwave you can automatically switch to a healthier diet. It is also compact, convenient, safe, and easy to use — making it most suitable for the elderly.

Home-made soups, sauces, fish, vegetable and meat dishes, rice and pasta, and desserts need no longer be a chore when cooking for one — as the recipe pages show.

Defrosting takes only minutes so you no longer have the excuse of forgetting to take an item out of the freezer. Snacks need no longer be made up of crisps, biscuits or chocolate. The microwave makes healthy snacks in no time at all. Reheating is no longer the chore it used to be, with loss of food value high on the agenda. The microwave reheats foods quickly and efficiently, often improving the flavour and texture of vegetables, casseroles and sauces, for example. It is particularly good at reheating small portions (i.e. for one) — and it is economical too.

With all these points in mind I have no doubt that, with the microwave, you will need to do far less thinking about, and planning for, a healthy diet. It is likely to come naturally!

6. USING THE RECIPES

Stirring And Turning Food In The Microwave
Foods cooked in the microwave need to be turned and/or
stirred to encourage even cooking. Where necessary the
recipe methods have included instructions for this.

Covering Food In The Microwave
Many foods need to be covered when cooking by microwave.
This is particularly relevant when cooking small quantities
since foods can dry out.

   Always use appropriate-sized containers which suit the
quantity of food being cooked. For example, do not try and
cook a small amount of soup in a large casserole — the large
surface area will cause excess evaporation and you will be
left with very little soup of unacceptable quality.

   So when do you cover food? When you want to keep
moisture in (e.g. soups, sauces, casseroles, vegetables,
puddings), cover with a lid or pierced cooking film (see page

20). When retaining moisture would spoil the dish (e.g.
reheating pastry dishes) or when it would make it too watery
(e.g. cooking the sauce around the Honeyed Spare Ribs on
page 69) leave it uncovered. If you are undecided about
covering or not covering, then it probably doesn't matter!
The recipes in the following pages include covering
instructions within the methods.

Cooking Times

All recipes in this book have been tested on 650W microwave
ovens. If your model differs in output, here is a guide to
adjusting the times. Remember though that cooking times
will vary according to the type of food, so do consider this
chart as a guide only. You can always check with the
manufacturer's instructions or with a similar recipe in your
instruction book.

600–700W	500–600W	400–500W
30 sec.	35 sec.	40 sec.
1 min.	1 min. 10 sec.	1 min. 20 sec.
5 min.	5 min. 45 sec.	6 min. 45 sec.
10 min.	11 min. 30 sec.	13 min. 30 sec.
20 min.	23 min.	27 min.
30 min.	34 min. 30 sec.	40 min. 30 sec.

Adjusting The Cooking Times To Suit The Number Of Portions

All the recipes in this book have been developed for one
person. It is a simple matter to double up on quantities if you
are cooking for two. In some cases it will be more practical to
cook one item at a time. If you decide to put twice the
quantity (or two items) into the microwave at one time, the
general rule is to add half the cooking time.

Here are extra *general* guides to adjusting the cooking
times of recipes which feed 2, 4 or 6 people. They may look
complicated at first, but once you get used to the idea it is
quite easy.

To reduce cooking times:
If a recipe states that 2 items/portions take 6 mins., divide by 3 (i.e. one extra portion). This gives you 2. Double this number to give you the cooking time for one item/portion (4 mins.). Add half this time (2 mins.) for each extra item/portion.

If a recipe states that 4 items/portions take 15 mins., divide by 5 (i.e. one extra portion). This gives you 3. Double this number to give you the cooking time for one item/portion (6 mins.). Add half the time (3 mins.) for each extra portion.

If a recipe states that 6 items/portions takes 28 mins., divide by 7. This gives you 4. Double it to give the time for one portion/item (8 mins.). Add 4 mins. for each extra item/portion.

To increase cooking times:
If a recipe serves one portion, add half the cooking time for each extra portion.

When using these guidelines, all timings are approximate. They will rarely work out as conveniently as the examples above. Remember it is better to underestimate the cooking time rather than to overcook. Items like rice, pasta and dried vegetables (i.e. those foods that will always need to absorb the same proportion of water) will take the same time to cook no matter what the quantity. Use the ingredient with the longest cooking time as a guide too.

Variable Powers
Most of the recipes are cooked on HIGH/100% power. Some recipes are better cooked on DEFROST/30%, MEDIUM/50% or MEDIUM-HIGH/70–75%. Check with your instruction book to see which setting coincides with these.

Symbols

Alongside the majority of recipes you will find the following information:

S: suitable for a snack
L: suitable for lunch or supper
M: suitable for a main meal
Easy: the recipe is simple to prepare
Needs a little extra care: the method may be a little long or detailed.

Standing Times

Microwave cooking generates heat within the food. It follows therefore that this heat will not disappear simply because the microwaves are switched off at the end of the cooking period. The food will go on cooking after it comes out of the oven and the standing times suggested in the recipes allow for this to happen and for the temperature in the food to even out. Do not make the mistake of missing out on this standing time if you want to achieve the best results.

Conversion Tables

Please keep to either metric or imperial measurements. The following conversion tables give equivalent measures rounded slightly up or down for convenience. All ingredients in this book were used at room temperature.

Capacities

1 fl oz	25ml
2 fl oz	50ml
¼ pt (5 fl oz)	150ml
½ pt (10 fl oz)	300ml
¾ pt (15 fl oz)	400ml
1 pt (20 fl oz)	500–600ml

Spoon Capacities

All spoon measures in this book are level.

¼ tsp	¼ x 5ml sp
½ tsp	½ x 5ml sp
1 tsp	5ml sp
2 tsp	2 x 5ml sp
1 tbsp	15ml sp

Weights

1 oz	25g
2 oz	50g
3 oz	75g
4 oz	100–125g
5 oz	150g
6 oz	175g
7 oz	200g
8 oz	225g
9 oz	250g
10 oz	275g
11 oz	300g
12 oz	350g
13 oz	375g
14 oz	400g
15 oz	425g
1 lb (16 oz)	450g
1½ lb	700g
2 lb	900g

7. BREAKFASTS

A nutritious breakfast, it has been proved, provides stamina and 'brain power' to last several hours. The microwave will make you a hot breakfast in minutes. Here are some ideas — check with the eggs section too on pages 95–101.

Fresh Coffee
Here is a useful tip if you enjoy coffee prepared by the filter or percolator methods. Instead of keeping it warm in the normal ways — for hours on a low heat — reheat individual cups or mugs in the microwave. One large cup or mug takes 1½–2 minutes on HIGH. Do not allow it to boil.

Instant Coffee
To make it in the microwave: heat a large cup or mug of water on HIGH until just boiling (1½–2 minutes). Leave room for it to bubble up and take care when taking it out of the oven as it can sometimes boil up unexpectedly. Stir in coffee powder or granules to taste.

Tea

Microwave a large cup or mug of water on HIGH until it boils (allow space for it to boil up and take care that it does not do this, just as you are taking it out of the oven). A large cup or mug takes $1\frac{1}{2}$–2 minutes to boil. Add a tea bag and allow it to stand until the required strength is reached.

Milk

150ml/$\frac{1}{4}$ pt milk for drinking or for cereals requires 1–$1\frac{1}{2}$ minutes on HIGH.

Croissants

Take care not to overheat croissants — they spoil easily. Try heating them on HIGH and on DEFROST/30% and see which you prefer. Sit the croissant(s) on a sheet of kitchen paper.

1 croissant takes about 15 seconds on HIGH
2 croissants take 20–25 seconds on HIGH
or
1 croissant takes about 20 seconds on DEFROST/30%
2 croissants take about 30 seconds on DEFROST/30%.

Hot Bread Roll

Heat a bread roll for breakfast (or refresh one going stale) on HIGH for 15–20 seconds or on MEDIUM/50% for 20–30 seconds. Check which method you prefer. It will taste freshly baked. Remember that if you heat more than one roll, add half the time per roll.

Poached Egg

Method

1. Microwave 150ml/$\frac{1}{4}$ pt water with a dash of vinegar in a small container on HIGH for 1 minute or until it boils.
2. Break an egg into the water and prick its yolk (it is important that the egg is at room temperature before use).
3. Cover and microwave on HIGH for 45 seconds then allow the egg to stand (and set) for 1–2 minutes before serving on toast or grilled frozen waffles.

Porridge   *Easy*

Total cooking time: 3–4 mins.

For a change add a 15ml sp/tbsp sultanas at stage 1.

Ingredients	Metric	Imperial
Porridge oats	50g	2 oz
Water (check with packet instructions) or milk and water	150ml	¼ pt

Method
1. Mix together the porridge oats and cold water in a deep, straight-sided container or bowl.
2. Microwave uncovered on HIGH for 3–4 minutes, stirring occasionally, until it boils.
3. When it boils, turn the power off and allow the porridge to stand for about 3 minutes before serving with sugar or salt.

Ham and Egg in Wholemeal Roll   *S/L Easy*

Total cooking time: about 1 min.

This makes a suitable snack at any time of the day. For breakfast, you may prefer to leave out the cheese.

Ingredients	Metric	Imperial
Egg, size 2 or 3, beaten	1	1
Milk	15ml	1 tbsp
Salt and pepper		
Butter or margarine	knob	knob
Ham slice, chopped	1	1
Wholemeal bap	1	1
Cheese	1 slice	1 slice

Method
1. Mix together the egg, milk and seasoning in a small microwave bowl and add the knob of butter.
2. Microwave the egg mixture on HIGH for 20 seconds and mix well with a fork.
3. Repeat stage 2 until the egg is almost set. Stir in the ham and let it stand, covered.
4. Slice the wholemeal bap and lay the cheese on the bottom half. Microwave the two halves on HIGH for 15–20 seconds.
5. Spoon the egg onto the cheese and top it with the top half of the bap.

Prune and Grapefruit Compote *Easy*

Total cooking time: 5 mins.

With the microwave there is no need to soak large dried fruit before cooking. Prepare this recipe the night before and chill it. Serve it on its own, with yoghurt or topped with muesli.

Ingredients	Metric	Imperial
Dried prunes	50g	2 oz
Apple juice	150ml	¼ pt
Grapefruit, peeled and segmented	1 small	1 small
Sugar (optional)		

Method
1. Microwave the prunes and apple juice in a covered container on HIGH for 5 minutes. Allow the fruit to cool, covered.
2. Mix the grapefruit segments with the prunes in their juice.
3. Stir in sugar to taste (optional).

Smoky Kedgeree   S/I Easy

Total cooking time: 16 mins.

This may be prepared the evening before and simply
reheated in the morning. Replace the mackerel fillets with
smoked cod or haddock if you prefer.

Ingredients	Metric	Imperial
Long grain brown rice	80g	3 oz
Vegetable oil	5ml sp	1 tsp
Water, boiling	225ml	8 fl oz
Grated rind and juice of lemon	½	½
Frozen smoked mackerel fillets,	75g	3 oz
defrosted on DEFROST/30%		
for 2–3 minutes		
(and stand for 5 minutes)		
Capers	5ml sp	1 tsp
Parsley, chopped	2 x 15ml sp	2 tbsp
Egg, hard-boiled or poached		
(see p. 33)	1 small	1 small

Method
1. Place the rice and vegetable oil in a large bowl. Stir well
   and pour the boiling water over.
2. Stir in the lemon juice and rind, cover and cook on HIGH
   for 15 minutes.
3. Allow the rice to stand for 5 minutes to finish cooking
   (and to absorb any water left in the container) before
   using.
4. Microwave the mackerel fillets in a covered container on
   MEDIUM/50% for 1 minute.
5. Flake the fish, removing any skin and bones and mix it
   into the rice with the remaining ingredients.

8. SOUPS, STARTERS & SAUCES

Fresh, dried or canned soups may be prepared in the microwave. For soups and sauces always use a container large enough to allow the liquid to boil up, particularly where milk is an ingredient. Stir soups and sauces a few times during cooking.

Lean Meat Pâté

S/L/M Easy

Total cooking time: 14–15 mins.

A tasty starter, snack or lunch that is quick and simple to prepare.

Ingredients	Metric	Imperial
Streaky bacon rashers, de-rinded	2	2
Chicken breast, boneless	75g	3 oz
Pork steak, boneless	100g	4 oz
Thyme, dried	pinch	pinch
Nutmeg, ground	pinch	pinch
Salt and ground black pepper		
Single cream or yoghurt	15ml sp	1 tbsp
Brandy	½–1 x 15ml sp	½–1 tbsp
Egg, size 5, beaten	1	1

Method

1. Stretch the bacon rashers with the back of a knife. Cut them and use them to line a small pudding dish.
2. Chop the meats roughly before mixing with the remaining ingredients.
3. Pour the mixture into the bacon-lined basin, pack down tightly and cover with pierced clear film.
4. Microwave on MEDIUM/50% for 14–15 minutes.
5. Drain off the liquid, cover with foil, place a weight on top and allow the pâté to cool before chilling and serving.

Sweetcorn Mousse   *S/L/M Needs a little extra care*

Total cooking time: 10–11 mins.

A delicately-flavoured mousse using a white sauce as a base. You will need a food processor or blender for this recipe.

Ingredients	Metric	Imperial
Sweetcorn kernels, defrosted on DEFROST/30% for about 2 minutes (and stand for 5 minutes) or drained canned	100g	4 oz
Spring onions, chopped	3	3
Butter or margarine	15g	½ oz
Plain flour	15g	½ oz
Milk	75ml	3 fl oz
Fresh white breadcrumbs	15ml sp	1 tbsp
Egg, size 5, beaten	1	1
Cayenne pepper	pinch	pinch
Salt and ground black pepper		
To garnish: chives, chopped		

Method
1. Place the sweetcorn and onions in a bowl, cover and microwave on HIGH for 3 minutes.
2. Whisk the butter, flour and milk together in a separate bowl. Microwave on HIGH for 2–3 minutes until the sauce thickens, stirring twice during cooking.
3. Stir the breadcrumbs into the sauce.
4. Blend the sweetcorn and onion for a few seconds (using a food processor or blender) and beat the mixture into the sauce with the egg, cayenne and seasoning.
5. Pour the mousse into a suitable bowl and microwave uncovered on MEDIUM/50% for about 5 minutes or until set.
6. Allow the mousse to stand for 10 minutes before turning out and garnishing with chopped chives. Serve with crispy bread, toast or biscuits.

Sweetcorn and Crispy Bacon Soup   *S/L/M Easy*

Total cooking time: 4–6 mins.

If cooking this soup in advance, add the bacon at the last minute only.

Ingredients	Metric	Imperial
Streaky bacon rasher	1	1
Spring onions, chopped	3	3
Bay leaf	1/2	1/2
Chicken stock	150ml	1/4 pt
Canned sweetcorn, drained	75g	3 oz
Cornflour	1/2 x 15ml sp	1/2 tbsp
Milk	3 x 15ml sp	3 tbsp
Salt and ground black pepper		

Method
1. Place the bacon rasher on a small rack on a plate and cover with a sheet of kitchen paper. Microwave on HIGH for 1 minute or until the bacon is crisp.
2. Place the spring onions, bay leaf, chicken stock and sweetcorn into a microwave container, cover and microwave on HIGH for 2 minutes, stirring once during the cooking.
3. Blend the cornflour with the milk and stir it into the sweetcorn mixture.
4. Cover and microwave on HIGH for 1–2 minutes.
5. Season to taste, remove the bay leaf, chop the crispy bacon and sprinkle over the dish before serving.

Quick Pea Soup   *S/L/M Easy*

Total cooking time: 5–6 mins.

Serve this soup with a good sprinkling of freshly ground black pepper.

Ingredients	Metric	Imperial
Spring onions, chopped	4	4
Butter or margarine	knob	knob
Potato, grated or chopped finely	50g	2 oz
Mint sauce, ready-made	2.5ml sp	1/2 tsp
Frozen peas	50g	2 oz
Chicken stock, hot	150ml	1/4 pt

Salt and ground black pepper
Milk   1–2 x 15ml sp   1–2 tbsp

Method
1. Place the onions, butter and potato in a small container, cover and microwave on HIGH for 2 minutes.
2. Stir in the mint sauce, frozen peas, hot chicken stock and seasoning. Cover and microwave on HIGH for 3 minutes.
3. Sieve, liquidise or purée the soup, then stir in the milk.
4. Reheat the soup on HIGH for 1 minute before serving if necessary.

Bacon and Olive Kebabs   *S/L/M Easy*

Total cooking time: 2 mins.

Use stuffed green olives and omit the red pepper if preferred.

Ingredients	Metric	Imperial
Streaky bacon rashers	2	2
Black olives	4	4
Red pepper, cut into small squares	1cm slice	½ inch slice

Method
1. Cut each bacon rasher into three and fold them loosely. Thread the bacon, olives and red pepper alternately onto two small wooden skewers.
2. Place the kebabs on a microwave rack on a plate and cover with a sheet of kitchen paper.
3. Microwave on HIGH for about 2 minutes or until the bacon is cooked.

Stock Pot   *Easy*

Total cooking time: about 13 mins.

The flavour of this speedy stock is better if cold water is used and brought up to the boil in the microwave rather than adding boiling water to the ingredients. Washed peelings (of root vegetables such as carrots, parsnips, swede etc.) can be used too. The stock can be used in the recipes for Lentil Soup (page 44) and Vegetable Casserole (page 87).

Ingredients	Metric	Imperial
Onion, sliced	small	small
Carrot, sliced	1	1
Celery, cut into pieces	1 stick	1 stick
Mushrooms, halved	2–3	2–3
Water	300ml	½ pt
Bay leaf	1	1
Parsley	few sprigs	few sprigs
Black peppercorns	6	6
Salt		

Method

1. Place all the ingredients with a little salt in a deep container, cover and bring to the boil on HIGH (about 3 minutes).
2. Once the mixture is boiling, microwave covered on MEDIUM-HIGH/75% for 10 minutes.
3. Remove the vegetables, and the stock is ready for use. Save the vegetables to serve in a white or cheese sauce (see page 47) and brown under the grill. Alternatively, purée them and use as a sauce with meat or fish.

French Onion Soup with Herb Croûtons

L/M Easy

Total cooking time: 10–11 mins.

This makes a filling dish. The croûtons can be prepared in advance and stored in a screw-top jar in a cool place for up to two weeks.

Ingredients	Metric	Imperial
Vegetable oil	5ml sp	1 tsp
Butter	small knob	small knob
Onions, sliced thinly	225g	8 oz
Dark brown sugar	5ml sp	1 tsp
Garlic clove, crushed	½–1	½–1
Water	150ml	¼ pt
Mushroom ketchup	15ml sp	1 tbsp
Worcestershire sauce	2.5ml sp	½ tsp
Salt and ground black pepper		
Slice of bread	1	1
Butter		
Mixed herbs, dried	¼ x 5ml sp	¼ tsp

Method

1. Place the vegetable oil, butter, onions and brown sugar into a deep container, cover and microwave on HIGH for 3 minutes.
2. Stir well and cook for another minute on HIGH.
3. Add the garlic, water, mushroom ketchup, Worcestershire sauce and seasoning to taste. Cover, microwave on HIGH for 5 minutes, stirring halfway through cooking, then allow the soup to stand covered for 5 minutes.
4. To prepare the croûtons, thinly spread the bread slice with butter and sprinkle the herbs over the butter.
5. Cut the bread into small cubes and spread them over a large plate.
6. Microwave the bread cubes uncovered on HIGH until they begin to crispen (1–1½ minutes). Rearrange them halfway through cooking. They will continue crispening as they cool.
7. Reheat the soup on HIGH for 1 minute if necessary, adding extra water if it is too thick.
8. Sprinkle the croûtons over the soup, then serve.

Lentil Soup   *L/M Easy*

Total cooking time: 25–30 mins.

Soups made with dried lentils are no longer a chore to make
for one person. The microwave eliminates sticky, burnt
pans, and the necessity for continuous checking and topping
up with liquid during cooking.

Ingredients	*Metric*	*Imperial*
Spring onions, chopped	4	4
Carrot, finely chopped	1	1
Bacon rasher, chopped	1	1
Water or stock (see page 41)	300ml	½ pt
Cumin, ground	pinch	pinch
Lentils	25g	1 oz
Salt and ground black pepper		
Lemon juice	5ml sp	1 tsp

Method
1. Place the onions, carrot and bacon into a deep container,
   cover and microwave on HIGH for 2 minutes.
2. Add the remaining ingredients, stir well and bring to the
   boil on HIGH (about 3–3½ minutes).
3. Microwave covered on MEDIUM/50% for 20–30 minutes or
   until the lentils are tender.
4. Liquidise or blend the soup adding extra liquid if required
   and adjust the seasoning if necessary.

Thick Vegetable Soup   *L/M Easy*

Total cooking time: 20–21 mins.

This is a good recipe for using up odds and ends in the store
cupboard or salad drawer of the fridge. The cooking time
can be cut down by microwaving on HIGH throughout.

Ingredients	Metric	Imperial
Butter or margarine	15g	½ oz
Onion, chopped	1 small	1 small
Potato, chopped	1 small	1 small
Parsnip, chopped	½ small	½ small
Carrot, chopped	1 small	1 small
Parsley, chopped	½ x 15ml sp	½ tbsp
Mixed herbs, dried	pinch	pinch
Nutmeg, ground		
Vegetable stock (see Stock Pot on page 41)	300ml	½ pt
Lettuce (outer leaves), shredded	15g	½ oz
Salt and ground black pepper		

Method

1. Put the butter, onion, potato, parsnip, and carrot in a deep container, cover and microwave on HIGH for 4 minutes.
2. Add the parsley, herbs, nutmeg to taste and the vegetable stock and bring to the boil on HIGH (about 3–3½ minutes).
3. Microwave covered on MEDIUM–HIGH/75% for 10 minutes (or on HIGH for 7–8 minutes) or until the vegetables are tender, stirring halfway through cooking.
4. Blend or liquidise the soup at this stage if liked.
5. Stir in the lettuce and seasoning to taste, cover and microwave on HIGH for 3 minutes.

Courgette and Carrot Soup with Tagliatelli

L/M Easy
Total cooking time: 13 mins.

A small amount of pasta (or use rice if you like) adds substance to this soup.

Ingredients	Metric	Imperial
Courgette, chopped finely	1 medium	1 medium
Carrot, chopped finely	1	1
Celery, chopped finely	1	1
Garlic clove, crushed	1	1
Butter or margarine	15g	½ oz
Stock or water	300ml	½ pt
Tomato purée	15ml sp	1 tbsp
Basil, dried	¼ x 5ml sp	¼ tsp
Salt and ground black pepper		
Tagliatelli, broken up	15g	½ oz
Milk	2–3 x 15ml sp	2–3 tbsp
Parsley, chopped	5ml sp	1 tsp

Method
1. Place the first five ingredients in a deep container, cover and microwave on HIGH for 3 minutes.
2. Add the stock or water, tomato purée, herbs, seasoning and tagliatelli, cover and microwave on HIGH for 10 minutes.
3. Stir in the milk and parsley and allow the soup to stand for 3 minutes before serving.

'Crostini' Bread Roll   *S/L/M Easy*

Total cooking time: 1–1½ mins.

This makes quite a substantial snack or starter. Take care not to overheat the roll or the crust will become rubbery.

Ingredients	Metric	Imperial
Butter	15g	½ oz
Garlic clove, crushed	½	½
Ground black pepper		
Bread roll	1	1
Cheese slices, thin	2	2
Ham slices, thin	2	2

Method
1. Soften the butter if necessary in a small bowl on DEFROST/30% for a few seconds.
2. Mix the garlic and black pepper to taste in the butter.
3. Cut the bread roll in two places, without taking the knife through the bottom crust. Spread half the butter in each slit.
4. Place a slice each of cheese and ham in each slit and press the roll together again.
5. Wrap the roll in a sheet of kitchen paper and microwave on DEFROST/30% for 1–1½ minutes or until the cheese has melted.

White Sauce   *S/L/M Easy*

Total cooking time: 2½–3½ mins.

Small quantities of sauces are simple to prepare in the microwave. Use a small bowl or jug.

Ingredients	*Metric*	*Imperial*
Butter	15g	½ oz
Flour	15g	½ oz
Milk	150ml	¼ pt
Salt and pepper		

Method
1. Microwave the butter on HIGH for about 30 seconds to melt it.
2. Stir in the flour then gradually add the milk, stirring well.
3. Microwave on HIGH for 2–3 minutes, stirring every 30 seconds, until the sauce is boiling and rising up the container.

Cheese Sauce: Add a pinch of dry mustard at stage 2, and 25–50g/1–2 oz grated cheese after stage 3. Allow the sauce to stand so that the cheese just melts into it.

Mushroom Sauce: Add 25g/1 oz finely sliced mushrooms after stage 1 and microwave, with the butter, on HIGH for 30 seconds before continuing with stage 2.

Onion Sauce: Add ½ small chopped onion or 2–3 chopped spring onions after stage 1. Microwave the onions and butter on HIGH for 1 minute before continuing with stage 2.

Parsley Sauce: Add ½ x 15ml sp/½ tbsp chopped parsley after stage 3.

Prawn Sauce: Add 25–40g/1–1½ oz peeled prawns and a little tomato purée after stage 3.

Poppadums

Brush both sides of a poppadum with cooking oil and place it on a sheet of non-stick or greaseproof paper. Microwave on HIGH for 1 minute. Two poppadums cook more evenly than one and take 1½ minutes (turn them around halfway through cooking).

9. FISH

If you have used a microwave before you will know that fish cooks beautifully by microwaves. If you have yet to try it, then do so as soon as possible!

CHECKPOINTS FOR FISH

★ Cover fish to keep in the juices. Microwave (roasting) bags and boil-in-the-bags are useful for this. Remember to pierce them to allow steam to escape.

★ Fish needs no liquid for cooking by microwaves. If you are making a sauce, use only sufficient liquid for this purpose.

★ Whole fish cook more evenly if the head and tail are wrapped in small pieces of smooth foil. Check with your instruction book regarding the use of foil. Make a slit in the skin each side of the fish to prevent it breaking open.

* Salt after cooking or the surface of the fish will dry out.

* When adding butter, melt it and brush it over the fish. This also encourages even cooking.

* Fish is cooked when the flakes separate easily. If the flesh inside is still slightly translucent, simply lay the flakes together again, cover the fish and allow it to stand for a few minutes. By this stage it should be cooked to perfection.

All the instructions in these recipes assume the fish has been gutted or prepared.

COOKING TIMES

	Weight	Minutes on HIGH	Standing time
Whole fish such as trout or mackerel	175g/6 oz	2–3	3–5 mins.
Fillet: thick	175g/6 oz	2–3	3–5 mins.
thin	100–150g/ 4–5 oz	1½–2	3–5 mins.

Cod and Lime Kebabs   *L/M Easy*

Total cooking time: 1½–2 mins.

Replace the lime with lemon if liked. Delicious as a starter or a light lunch with brown rice and salad.

Ingredients	Metric	Imperial
Cod portion, cut into 6 cubes	50g	2 oz
Lime slices, halved	2	2
Butter	15g	½ oz
Tarragon, dried	¼ x 5ml sp	½ tsp
Salt and freshly ground black pepper		

Method
1. Thread the cod cubes and lime slices alternately onto two small wooden skewers.
2. In a small container, microwave the butter on HIGH for 15–30 seconds or until melted. Brush the butter over the fish and lime.
3. Sprinkle the kebabs with the dried tarragon and place them on a small microwave rack on a plate.
4. Microwave uncovered on HIGH for 1–1½ minutes.
5. Sprinkle with salt and freshly ground black pepper and serve.

Salmon with Cucumber Sauce   *L/M Easy*

Total cooking time: 4½–6 mins.

Best results are obtained if the salmon and sauce are cooked separately.

Ingredients	Metric	Imperial
Butter	knob	knob
Cucumber, skin left on, and cut into small strips	40g	1½ oz
Tarragon, dried	¼–½ x 5ml sp + pinch	¼–½ tsp + pinch
Salt and ground black pepper		
Salmon steak	175g	6 oz
Spring onion, chopped	1	1
Cornflour	5ml sp	1 tsp
White wine vinegar or lemon juice	5ml sp	1 tsp
Cream or plain yoghurt	15ml sp	1 tbsp

Method

1. In a small jug melt the butter on HIGH for 20–30 seconds and stir in the cucumber, ¼–½ x 5ml sp/¼–½ tsp tarragon and seasoning.
2. Cover and cook on HIGH for 1 minute.
3. Place the salmon in a shallow container and sprinkle over the spring onion and the pinch of tarragon. Cover and microwave on HIGH for 2 minutes. Test the salmon by inserting a fork between the flakes. The flakes of the fish should separate quite easily. If the fish is slightly translucent in the centre, simply lay the flakes back in place, replace the cover and allow the fish to stand for a few minutes before continuing with stage 4.
4. Pour the fish juices into the cucumber and tarragon mixture then stir in the cornflour followed by the vinegar or lemon juice.
5. Microwave the sauce, uncovered, on HIGH and stirring every 30 seconds until it has thickened.
6. Stir the cream or yoghurt into the sauce and pour it over the salmon and serve.

Fish with a Spanish Flavour   *L/M Easy*

Total cooking time: 6–8 mins.

Make the sauce first, then you can cook the fish to perfection before coating it.

Ingredients	Metric	Imperial
Spring onions, chopped	3	3
Olive oil (optional)	5ml sp	1 tsp
Green (or red) pepper, chopped	½	½
Garlic clove, crushed	1	1
Tomato purée	2 x 15ml sp	2 tbsp
White wine or dry cider	5 x 15ml sp	5 tbsp
Salt and ground black pepper		
Black olives, chopped	3	3
Cod, haddock or hake fillet	175g	6 oz
Lemon juice	2 x 5ml sp	2 tsp

Method
1. Microwave the onions, olive oil (optional) and pepper on HIGH in a covered container for 2 minutes.
2. Stir in the garlic, tomato purée, wine or cider, and seasoning, and microwave, covered on HIGH for 2–3 minutes, stirring twice during cooking.
3. Add the black olives, cover and allow the sauce to stand while the fish cooks.
4. Place the fish in a shallow container and sprinkle over the lemon juice and some black pepper.
5. Cover and microwave on HIGH for 2 minutes. Test the fish as in stage 3 of the method of Salmon with Cucumber Sauce, opposite.
6. Pour the sauce over the fish (reheat on HIGH if necessary for ½–1 minute) and serve.

Smoked Haddock 'Crumble'   *S/L/M Easy*

Total cooking time: 7 mins.

The bran flakes make the crumble light, healthy and different.

Ingredients	Metric	Imperial
'Boil in the bag' smoked cod or haddock with butter, frozen	200g	7.05 oz
Parsley, chopped	5ml sp	1 tsp
Gherkin, chopped	1 small	1 small
Lemon or lime juice	5ml sp	1 tsp
Cream or yoghurt	2 x 15ml sp	2 tbsp
Salt and ground black pepper		
Bran flakes	15g	½ oz

Method
1. Place the frozen 'boil-in-the-bag' fish in a small shallow container. Slit the bag and cook on HIGH for 4–5 minutes.
2. Allow the fish to stand for 2 minutes before cutting the bag and turning the fish and butter out into the shallow

container. Discard the bag, any dividing paper and
bones, and flake the fish.
3. Stir in the remaining ingredients except the bran flakes
   and microwave covered on HIGH for 30 seconds.
4. Sprinkle the bran flakes over the fish mixture and
   microwave on HIGH for 30 seconds before serving
   immediately.

Trout with Butter and Mustard Sauce

L/M Easy

Total cooking time: 6½ mins.

Mustard complements the texture and flavour of trout
beautifully.

Ingredients	Metric	Imperial
Trout	175g	6 oz
Butter	25g	1 oz
Wine vinegar	5ml sp	1 tsp
Whole grain mustard, mixed	5ml sp	1 tsp
Black pepper		
Parsley to garnish		

Method
1. Wash and dry the cavity of the fish and slit the skin in two
   or three places to prevent it splitting open.
2. Place the trout in a shallow container, cover and
   microwave on HIGH for about 3 minutes (cover the head
   and tail with small areas of foil to prevent them
   overcooking — check with your manufacturer's instructions concerning the use of foil).
3. Drain and save the juices. Place the fish on a warm
   serving dish and allow it to stand while you prepare the
   sauce.
4. In the drained fish juices, microwave the butter on HIGH
   for 30 seconds.
5. Stir in the remaining ingredients, except the parsley, and
   microwave on HIGH for 1 minute.
6. Pour the sauce over the trout and serve with the garnish.

Prawns in Tomato Sauce   *L/M Easy*

Total cooking time: 7½ mins.

This quick and tasty treat will become a favourite. Delicious on a bed of rice or pasta ribbons.

Ingredients	Metric	Imperial
Onion, chopped	small	small
Garlic clove, crushed	1	1
Green pepper, chopped	15ml sp	1 tbsp
Can of tomatoes, chopped	200g	7 oz
Tabasco	2 drops	2 drops
Salt and ground black pepper		
Peeled prawns, defrosted on DEFROST/30% for 2–2½ minutes (and stand for 3 minutes)	100g	4 oz
Lemon juice	2 x 5ml sp	2 tsp

Method
1. Place the onion, garlic and green pepper into a container, cover and microwave on HIGH for 2 minutes.
2. Stir in the tomatoes, tabasco and seasoning and microwave covered for 5 minutes.
3. Add the prawns and lemon juice. Microwave uncovered on HIGH for 30 seconds.
4. Stir well, adjusting the seasoning, before serving.

Stir-Fry with Tuna   *L/M Easy*

Total cooking time: 7–8 mins.

This dish has more flavour if it is cooked in a browning dish. Don't miss out if you do not have one though!

Ingredients	Metric	Imperial
Vegetable oil	2 x 5ml sp	2 tsp
Onion, chopped	small	small
Garlic clove, crushed	1	1
Celery sticks, chopped	2	2
Green pepper, chopped	½	½
Button mushrooms, sliced	50g	2 oz
Sweetcorn, frozen	15ml sp	1 tbsp
Salt and ground black pepper		
Can of tuna fish, drained and flaked	184g	6½ oz
Lemon juice	15ml sp	1 tbsp
Parsley, chopped		

Method

1. Preheat a browning dish on HIGH for 5 minutes, add the oil and stir in the onion, garlic and celery. Cover and microwave on HIGH for 5 minutes, stirring once during cooking.

or

Place the oil, onion, garlic and celery in a container, cover and microwave on HIGH for 6 minutes, stirring once during cooking.

2. Allow it to stand covered for a few minutes before adding the pepper, mushrooms and sweetcorn. Cover and microwave on HIGH for 1 minute.

3. Season to taste and stir in the tuna flakes, lemon juice and parsley to taste.

4. Cover and microwave on HIGH for 1 minute.

Buttered Plaice with Capers   *L/M Easy*

Total cooking time: 3–4 mins.

The capers could be replaced with a 5ml sp/tsp of chopped fresh herbs for a simple but delicious flavour.

Ingredients	Metric	Imperial
Butter	25g	1 oz
Capers, drained	15–25g	½–1 oz
Parsley, chopped	5ml sp	1 tsp
Ground black pepper		
Plaice fillet	1 large	1 large
Lemon juice	5ml sp	1 tsp

Method

1. In a small container, microwave the butter for 30–45 seconds until it has melted.
2. Stir in the capers, parsley and black pepper to taste, and microwave covered for 30 seconds on HIGH.
3. Brush a little of the melted butter over the base of a shallow container and lay the plaice in it.
4. Brush over sufficient of the butter mixture just to coat the fish, cover and microwave on HIGH for 1–1½ minutes.
5. Reheat the rest of the butter mix on HIGH for 20–30 seconds and pour it over the plaice. Sprinkle over the lemon juice and allow the dish to stand, covered for 3 minutes.

Kippers with Tartare Sauce   S/L/M Easy

Total cooking time: 3½ mins.

This unusual flavour mix is very successful. Try serving this with scrambled egg (prepare in the microwave while the kippers stand — see method on page 97) and/or wholemeal bread.

Ingredients	Metric	Imperial
Kippers, boil-in-bag, defrosted on DEFROST/30% (pierce the bag) for 4–5 minutes (and stand for 5 minutes)	200g	7.05 oz
Tartare Sauce	2 x 5ml sp	2 tsp
Ground black pepper		

Method
1. Split the bag and place it in a shallow container.
2. Through the split, spread the tartare sauce over the kippers.
3. Microwave on HIGH for $3\frac{1}{2}$ minutes.
4. Allow the kippers to stand for 2–3 minutes before turning them out of the bag and sprinkling with black pepper to taste.

Sweet and Sour Prawns   *L/M Easy*

Total cooking time: 12–13 mins.

This will serve two as a starter. If you cannot get fresh beansprouts, simply reheat a can of drained beansprouts in a covered container on HIGH for 1–2 minutes at stage 3.

Ingredients	*Metric*	*Imperial*
Cornflour	2 x 5ml sp	2 tsp
Water	2 x 15ml sp	2 tbsp
Tomato ketchup	3 x 15ml sp	3 tbsp
Chilli sauce	2 x 5ml sp	2 tsp
Garlic clove, crushed	1	1
Prawns, defrosted on DEFROST/ 30% for 3–4 minutes (and stand for 5 minutes)	225g	8 oz
Lemon juice	5ml sp	1 tsp
Beansprouts	225g	8 oz
Soy sauce	15ml sp	1 tbsp

Method
1. In a deep bowl or container mix together the cornflour and water, then stir in the tomato ketchup, chilli sauce and garlic. Microwave on HIGH for 2–3 minutes, stirring two or three times, or until the mixture has thickened.
2. Stir in the prawns, cover and microwave on MEDIUM– HIGH/75% for 7 minutes, stirring once during cooking.

Stir in the lemon juice and allow to stand while the beansprouts are prepared.

3. Place the beansprouts in a large container with 30ml/ 2 tbsp water, cover and microwave on HIGH for about 3 minutes or until they are tender. Shake or stir them, halfway through cooking.
4. Drain the beansprouts and toss them in the soy sauce.
5. Serve the prawns in sauce on the bed of beansprouts.

Moules Marinière   *L/M Easy*

Total cooking time: 4½–5 mins.

Mussels are perfect for microwaving. Discard any which have not opened during cooking.

Ingredients	Metric	Imperial
Butter	15g	½ oz
Spring onions, chopped	3	3
Fresh mussels, soaked in several changes of water for at least 8 hours or overnight, scrubbed and beards scraped away	0.5 litre	1 pt
Ground black pepper		
Dry white wine	2–3 x 15ml sp	2–3 tbsp
Double cream	2 x 15ml sp	2 tbsp
Parsley, chopped		

Method
1. In a large container, microwave the butter on HIGH for 30 seconds or until melted.
2. Stir the onions into the butter, cover and microwave on HIGH for 1 minute.
3. Add the mussels, pepper and wine, cover and microwave on HIGH for 2½–3 minutes, shaking once or twice during cooking, until all the mussel shells have opened.

4, Use a slotted spoon to lift the mussels out of the juice and into a serving dish.

5. Stir the cream into the mussel juice and microwave on HIGH for 30 seconds.

6. Pour the sauce over the mussels and sprinkle with plenty of chopped parsley.

10. MEAT & POULTRY

The advantages of cooking small portions of meat in the microwave include speed, flavour retention and less shrinkage — particularly when the power level is turned down. Add to this the lack of messy frying pans and/or saucepans and you have some very good reasons for using the microwave to cook meat.

The only drawback is that small portions will not brown in the microwave. There are ways to overcome this — using microwave (roasting) bags to encourage browning, or finishing off under your grill (or the browning element in the microwave, if you have one). You will no doubt have also seen the variety of microwave browning powders on the market. In general these are very good but use them with caution for the first time as they tend to be highly flavoured. A browning dish is useful for cooking meat — you can sear the outside of the meat first and then finish cooking by microwave. A delicious method of browning meat and poultry in the microwave is to brush it with equal quantities of mustard, Worcestershire sauce and cooking oil before microwaving. Alternatively you may prefer to cook your meat under the conventional grill while you prepare the accompanying vegetables etc., in the microwave.

CHECKPOINTS FOR MEAT & POULTRY

* Even-shaped pieces cook best by microwaves. Help uneven pieces (like chicken legs or chops) to cook more evenly by wrapping the thin end with a small piece of smooth foil. Check with your manufacturer's instructions regarding the use of foil. The foil will reflect the microwaves, allowing that area to cook by conduction only.

* Minced meat should be stirred several times during cooking to break up the pieces.

* Cover meat and poultry during cooking, if only to save the oven walls from splashes.

* Salt pieces of meat after cooking or it will dry the surface, producing a tough result.

* When necessary, secure meat or poultry pieces with string or wooden (not metal) skewers.

* Cook pieces of meat or poultry on a rack in a shallow container. This makes sure that they do not sit (and 'stew') in their own juices during cooking, and that the microwaves can reach the meat from every angle. Cover with kitchen paper to absorb fat and steam, and prevent splashing on the oven walls.

* Turn meat pieces over, halfway through cooking, to encourage even results.

The following list gives suitable quantities of meat and poultry for a single portion, with the appropriate cooking and standing times. Times are given for cooking on HIGH.

Piece/Weight	Cooking time on HIGH	Standing time
Pork chop 175g/6 oz	4–4½ mins.	3–5 mins.
Lamb chop 175g/6 oz	3½–4 mins.	3–5 mins.
Bacon rashers, 2 back	2–2½ mins.	2 mins.
2 middle	3 mins.	2 mins.
2 streaky	2 mins.	2 mins.
Beefburgers, frozen, 2 x 50g/2 oz	3–4 mins.	3 mins.
Beefburgers, fresh, 2 x 100g/4 oz	5 mins.	5 mins.
Bacon chop, 175g/6 oz	3–3½ mins.	3 mins.
Gammon steak, 175g/6 oz snip the fat to prevent it curling up	3–3½ mins.	3 mins.
Liver, 100g/4 oz	2–3 mins.	2–3 mins.

Minced beef: follow method and times in a similar recipe (see Spicy Cottage Pie, page 67, and Bolognese, page 64)

Chicken joint, 175–200g/6–7 oz	4–5 mins.	5 mins.
Chicken drumsticks, 2	4–6 mins.	3 mins.

Duck portion: follow basic method in recipe page 79.

Steaks and sausages need slightly more gentle cooking and are better done on a browning dish (follow the manufacturer's instructions).

Weight	Cooking time on MEDIUM-HIGH 70–75%	Standing time
Steak 175g/6 oz, rare	1½–2½ mins.	3 mins.
Steak 175g/6 oz, medium	2½–3 mins.	3 mins.
Steak 175g/6 oz, well done	3–4 mins.	3 mins.
Sausages, 2 large, pricked	2–3 mins.	3 mins.

Chicken breasts also require more gentle cooking if they are not to toughen. Place the whole chicken breast in a small container, cover and microwave on MEDIUM/50% for 4–5 minutes or until the juice runs clear when the chicken is pierced with a skewer. Allow the chicken to stand, covered for 3 minutes before serving.

Less tender cuts of meat need long slow cooking even in the microwave. However you will still reduce the cooking time dramatically. It is a good idea to microwave on HIGH until the meat is hot then turn the power level down to MEDIUM/50% or DEFROST/30% until the meat is tender. Cooking times will depend on the quality of the meat, but check with a similar recipe in the following pages. Cut the meat into even-size pieces to encourage even cooking.

Bolognese Sauce   *L/M Easy*

Total cooking time: 19 mins.

Replace the carrot with mushrooms or green pepper if liked. Serve with spaghetti — see page 102.

Ingredients	Metric	Imperial
Onion, chopped	1 small	1 small
Streaky bacon (optional), de-rinded and chopped	1 rasher	1 rasher
Carrot, chopped	1 small	1 small
Beef, lean, minced	100g	4 oz
Tin of tomatoes, chopped	230g	8 oz
Mixed herbs	¼ x 5ml sp	¼ tsp
Garlic clove, crushed	½	½
Salt and pepper		

Method
1. Place the onion, bacon (optional), and carrot in a small, deep container, cover and microwave on HIGH for 2 minutes.
2. Stir in the minced beef, breaking it up with a fork. Cover and microwave on HIGH for 4 minutes, stirring once.

3. Stir in the remaining ingredients, cover and cook on HIGH for 3 minutes, stirring once. Cover and switch to MEDIUM/50% for about 10 minutes, stirring once or twice during cooking.

Beef Kebabs with Herbs
L/M Easy

Total cooking time: 2½–4 mins.

Always use wooden skewers when microwaving kebabs. Delicious served with lemon wedges, rice and a mixed salad.

Ingredients	Metric	Imperial
Minced beef, lean	100g	4 oz
Spring onions, finely chopped	3–4	3–4
Garlic granules	pinch	pinch
Fresh breadcrumbs	15g	½ oz
Tomato purée	2 x 5ml sp	2 tsp
Salt and ground black pepper		
Mixed herbs, dried	½ x 15ml sp	½ tbsp

Method
1. Mix together all the ingredients until they are combined, then divide the mixture into three portions.
2. Shape each portion into a 'sausage' around a wooden skewer, squeezing each on firmly so that it stays in place.
3. Put the kebab on a microwave rack on a plate and cook, uncovered, on HIGH for 2½–4 minutes. Turn the kebab over, halfway through cooking.

Chilli
L/M Easy

Total cooking time: 11 mins.

This dish is speedy to make. Use a can of prepared kidney beans. Adjust the quantity of chilli to suit your taste.

Ingredients	Metric	Imperial
Onion, chopped	1 small	1 small
Garlic clove, crushed	1	1
Red or green pepper, chopped	½	½
Lean minced beef	100g	4 oz
Can of red kidney beans, drained	125g	5 oz
Cumin, ground	pinch	pinch
Chilli powder	¼–1 x 5ml sp	¼–1 tsp
Tomato purée	15ml sp	1 tbsp
Red wine or water	15ml sp	1 tbsp
Salt and ground black pepper		

Method
1. Microwave the onion, garlic and red or green pepper in a covered container on HIGH for 2 minutes.
2. Stir in the remaining ingredients, cover and cook on HIGH for 3 minutes. Stir well.
3. Cover and microwave on MEDIUM–HIGH/75% for 6 minutes, stirring once during cooking.
4. Allow the dish to stand covered for 5 minutes before stirring and serving with crusty bread.

Bobouti

L/M Needs a little extra care

Total cooking time: 12 mins.

This rather special mince dish originates from South Africa.

Ingredients	Metric	Imperial
Brown bread	15g	½ oz
Milk	60ml	4 tbsp
Onion, chopped	1 small	1 small
Cooking oil	5ml sp	1 tsp
Minced beef, lean	100g	4 oz
Curry powder	½–1 x 5ml sp	½–1 tsp

Cinnamon, ground	¼ x 5ml sp	¼ tsp
Turmeric	¼ x 5ml sp	¼ tsp
Apricot jam	2 x 5ml sp	2 tsp
Seedless raisins	15g	½ oz
Lemon juice	5ml sp	1 tsp
Egg, size 3	1	1
Almond flavouring	2 drops	2 drops
Mustard powder	pinch	pinch
Salt and ground black pepper		

Method

1. Soak the bread in the milk for a few minutes.
2. Place the onion and cooking oil in a container, cover and microwave on HIGH for 2 minutes.
3. Stir in the minced beef, curry powder, cinnamon, turmeric, jam, raisins and lemon juice.
4. Squeeze out the bread, reserving the milk, and crumble it into the mince mix.
5. Microwave covered on HIGH for 5 minutes, stirring once or twice during cooking. Level the surface.
6. Mix the milk with the remaining ingredients and pour it over the mince.
7. Microwave on MEDIUM/50% for about 5 minutes or until the egg custard surface is set. Sprinkle with freshly ground black pepper or paprika and serve.

Spicy Cottage Pie   *L/M Easy*

Total cooking time: 19–20 mins.

This method saves the mashing process — cook the potato whole, slice it and layer it over the savoury mince base.

Ingredients	Metric	Imperial
Potato, scrubbed and pricked	175g	6 oz
Onion, chopped	1 small	1 small
Carrot, chopped	1 small	1 small
Vegetable oil	5ml sp	1 tsp
Minced beef, lean	100g	4 oz
Tomato purée	15ml sp	1 tbsp
Mixed herbs, dried	½ x 5ml sp	½ tsp
Water	15ml sp	1 tbsp
Worcestershire sauce	5ml sp	1 tsp
Mustard powder	5ml sp	1 tsp
Salt and ground black pepper		
Cheese, grated (optional)	25g	1 oz

Method

1. Microwave the potato on HIGH for 5–6 minutes, turning it over, halfway through cooking.
2. Wrap the potato in foil and allow it to stand while you prepare the mince base.
3. Place the onion, carrot and vegetable oil into a container, cover and microwave on HIGH for 2 minutes.
4. Stir in the minced beef, cover and microwave on HIGH for 2 minutes.
5. Stir well, add the remaining ingredients (except the cheese), cover and microwave on HIGH for 4 minutes.
6. Stir well, cover and switch to MEDIUM–HIGH/75% for 6 minutes.
7. Slice the potato and arrange the layers on top of the mince base.
8. Sprinkle with cheese and brown the surface under a hot grill (make sure the container is suitable).

Cheeseburger   *S/L Easy*

Total cooking time: 2–3 mins.

There is nothing as good as a home-made burger in a fresh bread roll. Here is a speedy version. The colour of the

burgers improves while they stand. Use a browning dish if
you prefer.

Ingredients	Metric	Imperial
Minced beef, lean	100g	4 oz
Onion, finely chopped	½ small	½ small
Bran flakes or corn flakes, crushed	25g	1 oz
Strong cheese, grated	25g	1 oz
Worcestershire sauce	5ml sp	1 tsp
Salt and ground black pepper		
Egg, beaten	15ml sp	1 tbsp

Method
1. Mix together all the ingredients and shape into two
   burgers.
2. Place the burgers on a microwave rack on a plate and
   cook on HIGH for 2–3 minutes, turning them over,
   halfway through cooking.
3. Allow the burgers to stand, covered, for 3 minutes before
   serving.

Honeyed Spare Ribs   *L/M Easy*

Total cooking time: 15–16 mins.

Serve these on a bed of rice with some raw spring onions.

Ingredients	Metric	Imperial
Pork spare ribs	350g	12 oz
Spring onions, chopped	2	2
Clear honey	15ml sp	1 tbsp
Dark soft brown sugar	½ x 15ml sp	½ tbsp
Worcestershire sauce	few drops	few drops
Tomato ketchup	2 x 5ml sp	2 tsp
French mustard	5ml sp	1 tsp
Ginger, ground	pinch	pinch
Mixed herbs, dried	pinch	pinch
Garlic powder	pinch	pinch

Method
1. Place the spare ribs in one layer in a shallow dish, cover and microwave on HIGH for 3 minutes. Drain and discard any fat.
2. Mix together the remaining ingredients and use it to coat the ribs well.
3. Microwave the ribs, covered, on HIGH for 3 minutes and baste them well.
4. Microwave, uncovered, on DEFROST/30% for 5 minutes, then baste well again.
5. Turn the power back up to HIGH and microwave uncovered for 4–5 minutes, stirring halfway through cooking. This should thicken the sauce so that it coats the ribs well.
6. Allow a standing time of 3–5 minutes before serving.

Pork with Apple and Walnut Stuffing   *L/M*

> *Needs a little extra care*
> *Total cooking time: 4–6 mins.*

For a thicker sauce, remove the pork after stage 5 and keep it covered. Stir in a 5ml sp/tsp of cornflour and bring to the boil on HIGH, stirring once or twice.

Ingredients	Metric	Imperial
Spring onions, chopped	2	2
Apple, cored and sliced	½	½
Walnuts, chopped	1–2 x 5ml sp	1–2 tsp
Salt and ground black pepper		
Dried sage	pinch	pinch
Pork steak, lean	175–225g	6–8 oz
Dry cider	120ml	4 fl oz

Method
1. In a small covered container microwave the onions, and apple on HIGH for 2 minutes, then stir in the walnuts, seasoning and sage. Allow the mixture to cool a little.

2. Place the pork between two sheets of greaseproof or non-stick paper and beat with a rolling pin until it is about 0.5cm/¼ inch thick.
3. Spread the stuffing over the pork, roll it up and secure with two wooden cocktail sticks. Cut the roll into two.
4. Place the rolls in a small container and pour in the cider.
5. Cover and microwave on MEDIUM/50% for 4–6 minutes or until the pork is tender and the juices run clear when pierced with a skewer.
6. Allow it to stand for 3 minutes before serving.

Bacon-Topped Potato   *L/M Easy*

Total cooking time: 5–8 mins.

The flavour of the bacon seeps into the potato. Choose a container into which the chop will fit snugly.

Ingredients	Metric	Imperial
Potato, sliced thinly	150–175g	6 oz
Spring onions, chopped	2–3	2–3
Ground black pepper		
Parsley, chopped	2 x 5ml sp	2 tsp
Stock, cider or water	15ml sp	1 tbsp
Bacon chop	1	1

Method
1. In a small deep bowl, layer the potato and onions, seasoning each layer with black pepper and one spoonful of the parsley.
2. Add the stock, cider or water and place the bacon chop on top, cover and microwave on HIGH for 6–8 minutes or until the potato is cooked in the centre — test with a skewer or sharp knife.
3. Sprinkle with the remaining parsley and allow the dish to stand, covered, for 3–5 minutes before serving.

Somerset Bacon   *L/M Easy*

Total cooking time: 6–6½ mins.

Choose a bacon chop with little fat. Vary the vegetable base
too.

Ingredients	Metric	Imperial
Leek, chopped	1	1
Carrot, cut into thin fingers	1	1
Sage	pinch	pinch
Apple juice or dry cider	4 x 15ml sp	4 tbsp
Black pepper, ground		
Bacon chop	1	1

Method
1. Microwave the leek, carrot, sage, apple juice and black
   pepper in a small covered container on HIGH for 3
   minutes. Stir well.
2. Place the bacon chop on top of the vegetables, cover and
   microwave on HIGH for 3–3½ minutes.
3. Allow the dish to stand, covered, for about 3 minutes
   before serving.

Bacon Hash   *S/L Easy*

Total cooking time: 9–10 mins.

Make the more usual corned beef hash by omitting the bacon
and stirring in 50–75g/2–3 oz flaked corned beef at stage 6.

Ingredients	Metric	Imperial
Potatoes, cut into chunks	225g	8 oz
Spring onions, chopped	2	2
Water	30ml	2 tbsp
Bacon rashers	2	2
Butter	15g	½ oz
Salt and ground black pepper		
Cheese, grated	25g	1 oz

Method
1. Place the potatoes in a container with the onions and water.
2. Cover the potatoes and microwave on HIGH for 5–6 minutes, stirring once during cooking.
3. Allow the potatoes to stand for a few minutes while you cook the bacon.
4. Place the bacon rashers on a microwave rack and cover them with a sheet of kitchen paper. Microwave on HIGH for 3 minutes or until the rashers are just beginning to crispen.
5. Mash the potatoes, with the onions and their cooking water, and the butter (use a fork for ease). Season to taste.
6. Cut the bacon into small pieces and stir these into the potato.
7. Place the mixture in a serving dish, sprinkle with cheese and microwave on HIGH for 1 minute. Alternatively, brown the surface under a hot grill if the container is suitable.

Chicken Curry   *L/M Easy*

Total cooking time: 10–11 mins.

Skin the chicken joint for this recipe if preferred. Serve with rice and a tomato, onion and lemon juice salad.

Ingredients	Metric	Imperial
Chicken joint	350g	12 oz
Cumin, ground	to taste	to taste
Coriander, ground	to taste	to taste
Onion, chopped	1 small	1 small
Garlic clove, crushed (optional)	1	1
Cooking oil	5ml sp	1 tsp
Curry powder	5ml sp	1 tsp
Turmeric	pinch	pinch
Natural yoghurt	3 x 15ml sp	3 tbsp
Tomato purée	5ml sp	1 tsp
Water	45ml	3 tbsp
Salt and ground black pepper		
Creamed coconut, grated	15g	½ oz

Method
1. Place the chicken in a container, sprinkle the cumin and coriander over, cover and microwave on HIGH for 5–6 minutes. Allow it to stand, covered for 5 minutes.
2. In another covered container microwave the onion, garlic, oil, curry powder and turmeric on HIGH for 2 minutes.
3. Stir in the yoghurt, tomato purée, water, salt and pepper and microwave, covered, on HIGH for a further 2 minutes.
4. Stir in the creamed coconut and pour the sauce over the chicken and its juices.
5. Microwave uncovered on HIGH for 1 minute and serve.

Spicy Chicken Drumsticks   *L/M Easy*

Total cooking time: 4 mins.

Remove the chicken skin if you like. Serve with rice and salad — delicious!

Ingredients	*Metric*	*Imperial*
Tomato purée	15ml sp	1 tbsp
French mustard	2 x 5ml sp	2 tsp
Chilli powder	pinch	pinch
Salt and ground black pepper		
Chicken drumsticks	2	2

Method
1. Mix together all the ingredients except the chicken.
2. Brush the drumsticks with the mixture and arrange them on a microwave rack on a plate — thin ends to the middle, or thin ends overlapping to encourage even cooking.
3. Cover with a sheet of greaseproof paper and microwave on HIGH for about 4 minutes or until the juices run clear when the chicken is pierced with a skewer.
4. Allow the chicken to stand for about 3 minutes before serving.

Chicken in Red Wine   *M Easy*

Total cooking time: 15–19 mins.

This classic dish is no longer a chore to prepare in small quantities.

Ingredients	Metric	Imperial
Chicken drumsticks	2	2
Small onions	100g	4 oz
Bacon rasher, de-rinded and chopped	1	1
Cloves, ground	pinch	pinch
Garlic granules	pinch	pinch
Plain flour	15ml sp	1 tbsp
Tomato purée	½ x 15ml sp	½ tbsp
Brandy (optional)	15ml	1 tbsp
Red wine	150ml	¼ pt
Mixed herbs, dried	pinch	pinch
Salt and ground black pepper		
Button mushrooms	50g	2 oz

Method

1. Arrange the drumsticks on a rack on a plate, thinner ends to the centre, or overlapping. Cover and microwave on HIGH for 4–6 minutes or until the juices run clear when the drumsticks are pierced with a skewer.
2. Pour the chicken juices into a bowl and add the onions, chopped bacon, cloves and garlic. Cover and microwave on HIGH for 3 minutes.
3. Stir in the flour, then add the tomato purée, brandy (optional), wine, mixed herbs and seasoning. Cover and cook for 3 minutes, stirring every minute until boiling.
4. Add the drumsticks and mushrooms, cover and microwave on DEFROST/30% for 5–7 minutes or until the chicken is tender.

Liver Stir Fry   *L/M Easy*

Total cooking time: 4–5 mins.

The speedy cooking of the microwave suits this dish.

Ingredients	Metric	Imperial
Soy sauce	½ x 15ml sp	½ tbsp
Wine vinegar	5ml sp	1 tsp
Sherry	5ml sp	1 tsp
Ginger, ground	good pinch	good pinch
Carrots, cut into 5cm/2 in sticks	100g	4 oz
Cornflour	5ml sp	1 tsp
Salt and ground black pepper		
Lamb's liver, cut into thin 5cm/2 in strips	100g	4 oz
Red pepper, seeds removed and sliced	½	½
Spring onions, cut into 5cm/2 in lengths	3	3

Method
1. Place the first five ingredients into a microwave container, cover and microwave on HIGH for 1 minute.
2. Season the cornflour with salt and ground black pepper and use it to coat the liver slices (this is easy if flour and liver are put into a small plastic bag and shaken).
3. Add the liver to the carrots, cover and microwave on HIGH for 1 minute.
4. Stir in the pepper and spring onions, cover and microwave on HIGH for 2–3 minutes, stirring once during cooking.
5. Allow to stand 2 minutes before serving.

Lemony Liver   *L/M Easy*

Total cooking time: 5 mins.

The liver is easy to slice into thin slivers when it is partially
frozen. Serve with rice or pasta.

Ingredients	*Metric*	*Imperial*
Butter (optional)	15g	½ oz
Onion, chopped	1 small	1 small
Lamb's liver, sliced into thin slivers	100g	4 oz
Salt and ground black pepper		
Lemon juice	15ml sp	1 tbsp
Parsley, chopped	15ml sp	1 tbsp

Method
1. Place the butter (optional) and onion into a container and
   microwave, covered, on HIGH for 2 minutes.
2. Stir in the liver and microwave on HIGH for about 3
   minutes, stirring every minute, or until the liver is just
   cooked.
3. Season to taste, stir in the lemon and parsley, and allow it
   to stand, covered, for 3–5 minutes before serving.

Minty Lamb Skewers   *L/M Easy*

Total cooking time: 5 mins. plus

Serve with plain yoghurt which has been flavoured with a
little chopped mint. It is also delicious with tomato sauce on
a bed of rice.

Ingredients	*Metric*	*Imperial*
Bread slice	1 small	1 small
Lamb, minced	175g	6 oz
Salt and ground black pepper		
Mint, finely chopped	2 x 15ml sp	2 tbsp
Egg, size 3 or 4, beaten	1	1

Method
1. Grate the bread slice to make breadcrumbs.
2. Place all the ingredients into a bowl and mix well.
3. Using your hands, shape the mixture around two wooden skewers and lay them on a microwave rack on a plate.
4. Cover with kitchen paper and microwave on MEDIUM/50% for 5 minutes or more — until the lamb is cooked to your liking.
5. Allow them to stand for 3 minutes before serving.

Honeyed Lamb with Rosemary   *L/M Easy*

Total cooking time: 3½–4 mins.

The flavour of this dish has to be tasted to be believed!

Ingredients	*Metric*	*Imperial*
Lamb chop	175g	6 oz
Garlic clove, sliced thinly	1 small	1 small
Honey	5ml sp	1 tsp
Soy sauce	5ml sp	1 tsp
Rosemary, fresh, or dried	1 sprig ½ x 5ml sp	1 sprig ½ tsp
Ground black pepper		

Method
1. Make a few slits in the chop and insert the garlic pieces. Place the chop in a small container.
2. Mix together the honey and soy sauce and brush the mixture over the lamb. Lay (or sprinkle) the rosemary on top and season with black pepper.
3. Cover and cook on HIGH for 3½–4 minutes and allow it to stand for 3–5 minutes before serving.

Tandoori Turkey   *L/M Easy*

Total cooking time: 2–2½ or 4–5 mins.

Flash the finished turkey under a hot grill for a brown appearance. Serve it with rice cooked with turmeric or saffron.

Ingredients	*Metric*	*Imperial*
Natural yoghurt	3 x 15ml sp	3 tbsp
Spring onions, chopped	2	2
Garlic clove, crushed	½	½
Root ginger, crushed	small piece	small piece
Chilli powder	good pinch	good pinch
Paprika	2.5ml sp	½ tsp
Garam masala	2.5ml sp	½ tsp
Lemon or lime juice	2.5ml sp	½ tsp
Turkey fillet	175g	6 oz

Method
1. Mix together all the ingredients except the turkey.
2. Make two or three slits in the turkey and pour the yoghurt mix over. Cover and allow it to marinade (in a cool place) for 2 hours or more.
3. Place the coated turkey on a small microwave rack on a plate and microwave uncovered on HIGH for 2–2½ minutes or on MEDIUM/50% for 4–5 minutes (or until the juices run clear when the turkey is pierced with a skewer).
4. Cover with foil and allow the turkey to stand for 5 minutes before serving.

Duck with Fruity Sauce   *M Needs a little extra care*

Total cooking time: about 10 mins.

The redcurrant jelly may be replaced by the more conventional cherries or plums (use canned, drained and stoned). Alternatively use a thick, old-fashioned-style marmalade for a tangy orange sauce — and use orange juice instead of red wine.

Ingredients	Metric	Imperial
Duck joint	350g	12 oz
Spring onions, chopped	3–4	3–4
Butter or margarine	knob	knob
Button mushrooms, sliced thinly	25g	1 oz
Mixed herbs, dried	pinch	pinch
Tomato purée	½ x 15ml sp	½ tbsp
Redcurrant jelly	2 x 15ml sp	2 tbsp
Salt and ground black pepper		
Cornflour	5ml sp	1 tsp
Red wine or stock	2 x 15ml sp	2 tbsp

Method
1. Place the duck on a microwave rack in a shallow container and microwave covered for 2 minutes on HIGH.
2. Microwave covered on DEFROST/30% for a further 4 minutes then drain off any fat which has collected in the container.
3. Cover and continue microwaving on DEFROST/30% for a further 2 minutes.
4. Drain off the fat and juice, cover and allow the duck to stand for 3–5 minutes.
5. Meanwhile place the onions, butter, mushrooms and mixed herbs in a small container, cover and microwave on HIGH for 1 minute.
6. Stir in the remaining ingredients in the order listed then microwave uncovered on HIGH for 1 minute or until thickened. Stir at least once during cooking.
7. Crisp the duck skin quickly under a hot grill before spooning the sauce over it.

11. VEGETABLES & VEGETABLE DISHES

Vegetables cooked in the microwave retain maximum colour and flavour, and can be cooked to produce a texture which is soft or which has 'a bite' to suit your own preference. Small portions cook well in the microwave. Always use a container which leaves 2½cm/1 inch headroom (no more). The main fault which occurs when cooking small quantities of vegetables is using too large a container.

The microwave is ideal for cooking meatless meals too. The next few pages contain some interesting recipes for you to try.

CHECKPOINTS FOR VEGETABLES
★ Use good quality vegetables for good results.

★ Personal taste will dictate cooking times — according to whether you like your vegetables with 'a bite' or whether you like them soft.

* 30ml/2 tbsp is sufficient water to cook most vegetables.

* Always cover vegetables during cooking to retain maximum moisture.

* Prick the skins of whole vegetables such as potatoes or courgettes, to prevent them bursting.

* Cut vegetables into small, even, pieces for the best results.

* Stir or shake vegetables at least once during cooking.

* Salt vegetables after cooking or it will cause their surfaces to dry and toughen.

* When using microwave (roasting) bags or boil-in-the-bags, tie them loosely or pierce them in a convenient place to allow steam to escape.

* Generally, frozen vegetables need no defrosting before cooking in the microwave.

Cooking and standing should be completed in a small covered container or in a small roasting/microwave/boil-in bag. Rearrange, stir or shake vegetables halfway through cooking for best results. If wished, add salt after cooking and before standing.

FRESH VEGETABLES
The following list gives suitable quantities of vegetables for a single portion, with the appropriate cooking and standing times.

Vegetable	Amount	Add water	Cooking time on HIGH	Standing time
Artichoke:				
globe	1	30ml/2 tbsp	4–6 mins.	3–4 mins.
Jerusalem	100g/4 oz	15ml/1 tbsp	3–4 mins.	3 mins.
Asparagus	100g/4 oz	15ml/1 tbsp	3 mins.	3–4 mins.
Aubergine	1 small, cubed	30ml/2 tbsp	2–3 mins.	3 mins.

Vegetable	Amount	Add water	Cooking time on HIGH	Standing time
Beans: broad	100g/4oz	30ml/2 tbsp	3–4 mins.	3 mins.
runner	100g/4 oz	30ml/2 tbsp	3–4 mins.	3 mins.
whole	100g/4 oz	30ml/2 tbsp	3–5 mins.	3–5 mins.
Beansprouts	75g/3 oz	knob butter	1–2 mins.	2–3 mins.
Beetroot	1 medium	to cover	5–6 mins.	5 mins.
Broccoli small florets	100g/4 oz	45ml/3 tbsp	3–5 mins.	5 mins.
Brussels sprouts	100g/4 oz	30ml/2 tbsp	2–4 mins.	3 mins.
Cabbage	100g/4 oz shredded	15–30ml/ 1–2 tbsp	3–4 mins.	3 mins.
Carrots	100g/4 oz sliced	15–30ml/ 1–2 tbsp	3–4 mins.	3 mins.
Cauliflower	100g/4 oz florets	30ml/2 tbsp	3 mins.	3 mins.
Celery	100g/4 oz	30ml/2 tbsp	3–4 mins.	3 mins.
Corn on the cob	1	brush with melted butter	3 mins.	3–5 mins.
Courgettes	100g/4 oz	15ml/1 tbsp	3 mins.	3 mins.
Leeks	100g/4 oz	15ml/1 tbsp	3 mins.	3 mins.
Marrow	100g/4 oz cubed	15ml/1 tbsp	3 mins.	3 mins.
Mushrooms	50g/2 oz	5ml/1 tsp or knob butter	1 min.	1–2 mins.
Onions	1 medium, sliced	5ml/1 tsp or knob butter	2–3 mins.	2–3 mins.
	1 large, whole	15ml/1 tbsp	2–2½ mins.	3–5 mins.
Parsnips	100g/4 oz	15ml/1 tbsp	3 mins.	3 mins.
Peas	100g/4 oz	15ml/1 tbsp or knob butter, if liked	2–3 mins.	3 mins.
Potato, old	175g/6 oz whole, pricked		5–6 mins.	5 mins.
	cubed	15ml/1 tbsp	3 mins.	3 mins.
new	100g/4 oz	15ml/1 tbsp	2½–3½ mins.	3–5 mins.
Spinach	100g/4 oz	shake off excess water	2–3 mins.	3 mins.
Swede	100g/4 oz cubed	15ml/1 tbsp	4–5 mins.	3–5 mins.
Tomato	1 large	knob butter, if liked	1–1½ mins.	? mins.
Turnips	100g/4 oz	30ml/2 tbsp	3–5 mins.	3 mins.

Courgettes, Greek-Style   *L/M Easy*

Total cooking time: 8½–9½ mins.

This dish makes a meal in itself when sprinkled with plenty of grated cheese. As a vegetable accompaniment it is delicious served hot or cold with meat or fish.

Ingredients	Metric	Imperial
Butter or margarine	15g	½ oz
Courgettes, sliced	100g	4 oz
Garlic clove, crushed	½	½
Tin of tomatoes	230g	8 oz
Mushrooms, sliced	25g	1 oz
Salt and ground black pepper		
Oregano, fresh chopped, or	5ml sp	1 tsp
dried	2.5ml sp	½ tsp

Method
1. Melt the butter or margarine on HIGH for 20–30 seconds.
2. Stir in the courgettes and garlic, cover and microwave on HIGH for 2 minutes then stir well.
3. Add the remaining ingredients, stir well, cover and microwave on HIGH for 6–7 minutes. Stir once during cooking.
4. Allow to stand, covered, for 5 minutes before serving.

Mushrooms à la Greque   *S/L/M Easy*

Total cooking time: 2–3 mins.

This is delicious as a snack on toast or as a starter with crunchy French bread or croûtons.

Ingredients	Metric	Imperial
Button mushrooms	100g	4 oz
Can of tomatoes, chopped	230g	8 oz
Cornflour	5ml sp	1 tsp
Garlic granules	pinch	pinch
Sugar	pinch	pinch
Bay leaf, crushed	½	½
Basil, dried	pinch	pinch
Salt and ground black pepper		

Method
1. Microwave all the ingredients in a covered container on HIGH for 2 minutes, stirring halfway through cooking.
2. Taste the sauce to check that the cornflour is cooked. If it still tastes 'starchy' microwave for a further 30 seconds on HIGH.

Tasty Layered Potato   *S/L/M Easy*

Total cooking time: 5½–6½ mins.

This dish tastes better if the potatoes are scrubbed and the peel is left on. A sprinkling of grated cheese added at stage 5, makes this a meal in itself.

Ingredients	Metric	Imperial
Potatoes, scrubbed and finely sliced	175g	6 oz
Onion, finely sliced	1 small	1 small
Salt and ground black pepper		
Dill weed, dried	to taste	to taste
Milk	2 x 15ml sp	2 tbsp
Butter or margarine (optional)	15g	½ oz

Method
1. Arrange layers of potatoes and onion, alternately in a small deep container, seasoning each layer with salt and

pepper and dill weed to taste. Finish with a layer of potatoes.
2. Spoon the milk over the potatoes.
3. In a small container melt the butter (optional) on HIGH for 15–30 seconds and then brush it over the top of the potatoes.
4. Cover and microwave on HIGH for 5–6 minutes or until the potatoes feel soft when pierced with a knife.
5. If the container is suitable, brown the top of the potatoes under a hot grill.

Pepper with Cheese   *L/M Easy*

Total cooking time: about 5 mins.

Here is a basic recipe for stuffed peppers. Vary the ingredients to suit your taste.

Ingredients	Metric	Imperial
Red, green or yellow pepper, halved lengthways and de-seeded	1 x 150g	1 x 5 oz
Rice, cooked (see page 103)	50g	2 oz
Spring onion, chopped	1	1
Sultanas	15g	½ oz
Cheese, mature, grated	25g	1 oz
Natural yoghurt	15ml	1 tbsp
Mixed spice	¼ x 5ml sp	¼ tsp
French mustard	5ml sp	1 tsp
Salt and ground black pepper		

Method
1. Lie the pepper halves in a container and pour 15ml/1 tbsp water around. Cover and microwave on HIGH for 2 minutes.
2. Mix together the remaining ingredients and use the mixture to fill the drained pepper halves.
3. Cover and microwave on HIGH for about 3 minutes or until the filling is heated through.

Vegetable Casserole   *L/M Easy*

Total cooking time: 11½–14½ mins.

Vary the vegetable mixture according to the season. Try it using frozen vegetables too.

Ingredients	Metric	Imperial
Butter or margarine	15g	½ oz
Onion, sliced thinly	small	small
Flour	2 x 5ml sp	2 tsp
Nutmeg	¼ x 5ml sp	¼ tsp
Stock, chicken or vegetable (see page 41) or a mixture of stock and milk	150ml	¼ pt
Cheese, grated	40g	1½ oz
Salt and ground black pepper		
Potatoes, sliced thinly	110g	4 oz
Carrot, sliced thinly	small	small
Peas	25g	1 oz
Tomato, sliced	1	1

Method

1. Microwave the butter on HIGH in a small bowl for 30 seconds or until melted.
2. Stir in the onion slices, cover and microwave on HIGH for 1 minute.
3. Stir in the flour, nutmeg and stock. Microwave on HIGH, stirring once or twice, until the sauce boils (2–3 minutes).
4. Stir in the cheese and season to taste.
5. In a small, straight-sided container, layer the potatoes, carrot, peas and tomato (save one tomato slice to garnish) and top them with the sauce.
6. Microwave uncovered on HIGH for 8–10 minutes or until the potatoes are cooked in the centre (use a knife to test).
7. Allow the dish to stand for 3–5 minutes before garnishing with the tomato slice and serving.

Onion with Stilton and Walnuts   *S/L/M Easy*

Total cooking time: 4 mins. + grilling

This dish really needs a grill to give it an attractive appearance, so use a suitable container.

Ingredients	Metric	Imperial
Onion, chopped roughly	medium	medium
Water	5ml	1 tsp
Apple, cored and sliced	½	½
Walnuts, chopped	15ml sp	1 tbsp
Ground black pepper		
Stilton cheese, crumbled	15–25g	½–1 oz

Method

1. Place the onion in a small container with the water, cover and microwave on HIGH for 3 minutes, stirring once during cooking.
2. Allow the onion to stand for 2–3 minutes before draining off the liquid and mixing in the apple, walnuts and black pepper.
3. Sprinkle the crumbled Stilton over the top and microwave on HIGH for 1 minute.
4. Brown under a hot grill before serving.

Cheesy Broccoli   *L/M Easy*

Total cooking time: 6–7 mins.

Omit the ham and add extra cheese to make it a meatless dish.

Ingredients	Metric	Imperial
Broccoli, cut into small florets	100g	4 oz
Water	2 x 15ml sp	2 tbsp
Flour	15g	½ oz
Milk	150ml	¼ pt
Butter	15g	½ oz

Mustard, prepared	½ x 5ml sp	½ tsp
Ham, cut into thin strips	1 slice	1 slice
Parmesan cheese, grated	15ml sp	1 tbsp
Ground black pepper		

Method
1. Place the broccoli in a small container, add the water, cover and microwave on HIGH for about 4 minutes or until it is just cooked.
2. Allow the broccoli to stand while you make the sauce.
3. Place the flour in a jug and gradually stir in the milk. Add the butter and mustard and microwave on HIGH for 2–3 minutes, stirring once or twice, or until the sauce is thickened and cooked.
4. Stir in the ham, cheese (save a little for sprinkling over the finished surface) and seasoning.
5. Drain the broccoli and pour the sauce over it. Sprinkle with the remaining cheese and brown under a hot grill if liked (make sure the container is suitable).

Gingered Cabbage   *L/M Easy*

Total cooking time: 5 mins.

Use fresh, chopped root ginger if you wish. Take care that it does not 'lump together' in one piece. Add some chopped crispy bacon to add 'bite'. Use the rest of the cabbage to make Cabbage with Ham and Yoghurt on page 93.

Ingredients	*Metric*	*Imperial*
Butter	15g	½ oz
Cabbage, shredded	100g	4 oz
Ginger, ground	¼ x 5ml sp	¼ tsp
Salt and ground black pepper		

Method
1. Melt the butter on HIGH for about 30 seconds.
2. Stir in the cabbage and ginger, cover and microwave on

HIGH for about 4 minutes, stirring once, or until the cabbage is just cooked.
3. Season to taste and allow the dish to stand, covered, for 3 minutes before serving.

Baked Vegetables

L/M Easy

Total cooking time: 6 mins.

Use courgettes or parsnips in this recipe to ring the changes.

Ingredients	Metric	Imperial
Carrot, sliced	small	small
Celery, cut into thin strips	stick	stick
Spring onion, chopped	1	1
Cauliflower, small florets	few florets	few florets
Fennel seeds	pinch	pinch
Water	2 x 5ml sp	2 tsp
Lemon juice	2 x 5ml sp	2 tsp
Salt and ground black pepper		
Cheese, grated	25g	1 oz

Method
1. Place the vegetables in a container, sprinkle with the fennel seeds and pour the water and lemon juice over them.
2. Cover and microwave on HIGH for about 5 minutes (stirring or shaking once or twice) or until the vegetables are just cooked.
3. Allow them to stand for 3 minutes before draining off the liquid, seasoning to taste and sprinkling the cheese over.
4. Either microwave on HIGH for ½–1 minute until the cheese has melted,
or
    if the dish is suitable, lightly brown the cheese topping under a hot grill.

Corn-on-the-cob with Garlic Butter

S/L/M Easy

Total cooking time: 6–7 mins.

The quantity of butter can be varied according to taste.

Ingredients	Metric	Imperial
Butter	25g	1 oz
Garlic clove, crushed	1	1
Cob of corn	1 medium	1 medium
Parsley, chopped or other fresh herb	5ml sp	1 tsp

Method
1. Place half the butter with the crushed garlic in a small container and microwave on HIGH for 30 seconds or until melted.
2. Brush the butter over the corn then wrap it in non-stick or greaseproof paper.
3. Place the parcel on a plate and microwave on HIGH for 5–6 minutes or until cooked.
4. Sprinkle the parsley over and allow the corn to stand for 3 minutes before melting the remaining butter over the top and serving it.

Stuffed Tomato

L/M Easy

Total cooking time: 4 mins.

Try using left-over cooked rice, bulgar wheat or pulses to replace the bran flakes.

Ingredients	Metric	Imperial
Beef tomato	1	1
Spring onions, chopped	4	4
Garlic granules	pinch	pinch
Vegetable oil	5ml	1 tsp
Green pepper, de-seeded, chopped	½	½
Raisins	15g	½ oz
Walnuts, chopped	15g	½ oz
Garam masala or curry powder	¼–½ x 5ml sp	¼–½ tsp
Worcestershire sauce	dash	dash
Bran flakes	15g	½ oz
Salt and ground black pepper		

Method

1. Slice the top off the tomato and scoop out the centre. Chop the contents.
2. Place the spring onions, garlic, vegetable oil, green pepper and raisins into a microwave bowl, cover and microwave on HIGH for 2 minutes.
3. Stir in the remaining ingredients and the chopped tomato and microwave on HIGH for 1 minute.
4. Pile the mixture back into the tomato and top it with its lid.
5. Place the stuffed tomato on a plate and microwave on HIGH for 1 minute.
6. Stand the tomato for 2 minutes, covered, before serving.

Spinach and Cheese Stuffed Potato   *L/M Easy*

Total cooking time: 11–12 mins.

The jacket potato makes one of the speediest meals for one. The addition of spinach and cheese makes it a substantial meal.

Ingredients	Metric	Imperial
Potato, scrubbed and pricked	1 x 225g	1 x 8oz
Spinach, frozen	100g	4 oz
Butter or margarine	25g	1 oz
Salt and ground black pepper		
Cheddar cheese, grated	25g	1 oz
Natural yoghurt	2 x 15ml sp	2 tbsp
Parsley, chopped	5ml sp	1 tsp
Chives, chopped	5ml sp	1 tsp
Nutmeg, grated	pinch	pinch

Method

1. Wrap the potato in a sheet of kitchen paper and microwave on HIGH for 6–7 minutes. Halfway through cooking, turn it over. Allow it to stand for 5 minutes.
2. Microwave the spinach in a covered container for 5 minutes on HIGH, stirring halfway through cooking. Allow it to stand for 3 minutes before draining and stirring in half the butter or margarine and seasoning with salt and black pepper.
3. Cut the potato in half lengthways and scoop out the flesh.
4. Mash the scooped-out potato with the rest of the butter or margarine and stir in the cheese, yoghurt, parsley, chives, nutmeg and seasoning.
5. Pile the mixture back into the potato halves and sit them on the bed of spinach to serve.

Cabbage with Ham and Yoghurt   *L/M Easy*

Total cooking time: 4–5 mins.

Use the rest of the cabbage to make Gingered Cabbage on page 89. Use soured cream instead of yoghurt if liked.

Ingredients	Metric	Imperial
Butter	15g	½ oz
Cabbage, shredded	100g	4 oz
Spring onions, chopped	3	3
Salt		
Paprika	¼ x 5ml sp	¼ tsp
Ham, chopped	25g	1 oz
Natural yoghurt	1–2 x 15ml sp	1–2 tbsp

Method
1. Melt the butter on HIGH for about 30 seconds.
2. Stir in the cabbage and spring onions, cover and microwave on HIGH for 3–4 minutes, stirring once, or until the cabbage is just cooked.
3. Season with salt and paprika and stir in the ham. Microwave, covered, on HIGH for 30 seconds.
4. Allow the cabbage to stand, covered, for 3 minutes before serving, topped with the yoghurt.

12. CHEESE & EGGS

Cheese and egg dishes can easily overcook and become hard or stringy during any form of cooking. For this reason it is a good idea to melt cheese in the microwave on DEFROST/30%.

Eggs may be poached (see Breakfast section, page 33), scrambled, baked and made into omelettes in the microwave, but do not attempt to cook an egg in its shell. It can be positively dangerous as the shell explodes!

Cheese-Topped Baked Eggs *S/L Easy*

Total cooking time: 1–1½ mins. + grilling

A simple, delicious dish served with wholewheat or granary bread. Use the grill to achieve a perfect finish — make sure your containers are suitable.

Ingredients	Metric	Imperial
Eggs, size 2	2	2
Dill weed	pinch	pinch
Salt and ground black pepper		
Cheddar or Gruyère Cheese, grated	25g	1 oz

Method

1. Break the eggs into two ramekins or small dishes and pierce the yolks.
2. Sprinkle the dill weed over each egg and microwave both containers, covered with kitchen paper, on MEDIUM/50% for 1–1½ minutes or until the eggs are slightly undercooked.
3. Season to taste with salt and pepper and sprinkle the grated cheese over the eggs.
4. Place under a hot grill until the cheese bubbles then serve immediately.

Egg and Leek Pot   S/L Easy

Total cooking time: 3½–5 mins.

Another dish suitable for serving with wholewheat or granary bread.

Ingredients	Metric	Imperial
Leek, chopped finely	1 small	1 small
Butter or margarine	knob	knob
Eggs, size 2 or 3, beaten	2	2
Mace, ground	pinch	pinch
Salt and ground black pepper		
Chives, chopped	2 x 5ml sp	2 tsp

Method

1. Place the leek and butter into a small shallow container, cover and microwave on HIGH for 2–3 minutes.
2. Stir the leeks. Mix the beaten eggs with the mace and

seasoning to taste.

3. Pour the egg mixture over the leeks, cover with kitchen paper and microwave on MEDIUM/50% for about 1½–2 minutes or until the eggs are just set.

4. Sprinkle with chives and allow the eggs to stand covered for 2 minutes before serving.

Scrambled Eggs with Herb and Garlic Cheese

S/L Easy

Total cooking time: 2–3 mins.

Use a ready-prepared cream cheese for this recipe or mix plain cream cheese with your favourite herbs and some crushed garlic.

Ingredients	Metric	Imperial
Eggs, size 2, beaten	2	2
Salt and ground black pepper		
Milk	15ml sp	1 tbsp
Butter or margarine	15g	½ oz
Cream cheese with herbs and garlic	40g	1½ oz

Method

1. Mix together the eggs, seasoning, milk and butter in a bowl and microwave on HIGH for 1 minute, stirring halfway through cooking.

2. Crumble in the cream cheese and continue cooking on HIGH, stirring every 30 seconds until the creamy mixture is almost cooked.

3. Allow the eggs to stand covered for 1 minute — they will set during this time.

Scrambled Eggs with Mushroom and Cheese

S/L Easy

Total cooking time: 2–3½ mins.

Simply serve on toast.

Ingredients	Metric	Imperial
Button mushrooms, sliced	50g	2 oz
Butter or margarine	15g	½ oz
Eggs, size 2, beaten	2	2
Milk	15ml sp	1 tbsp
Salt and ground black pepper		
Cheese, grated	25g	1 oz
Chives, chopped	5ml sp	1 tsp

Method
1. Place the mushrooms and butter in a bowl, cover and microwave on HIGH for 1 minute.
2. Mix together the eggs, milk and seasoning and pour the mixture over the mushrooms.
3. Microwave uncovered on HIGH, stirring every 30 seconds until the egg is slightly undercooked.
4. Stir in the grated cheese and chives and microwave on HIGH for a further 30 seconds.
5. Allow to stand covered for 1 minute before serving.

Spinach-filled Omelette

S/L Easy

Total cooking time: 6–7 mins.

Spinach and eggs make good partners. The nutmeg adds a special flavour to the filling. Instead of nutmeg you could add a good sprinkling of Parmesan cheese.

Ingredients	Metric	Imperial
Spinach, frozen	50g	2 oz
Butter	15g	½ oz
Salt and ground black pepper		
Nutmeg	pinch	pinch
Eggs, size 2 or 3, beaten		
Milk	2 x 15ml sp	2 tbsp

Method
1. In a small covered container, microwave the spinach on HIGH for 4 minutes. Stir well, drain off the liquid, stir in half the butter and season with salt and black pepper and nutmeg.
2. In an 18cm/7 in shallow round container, melt the rest of the butter on HIGH for 30 seconds. Tilt the container to spread the butter over its base.
3. Mix together the eggs and milk with a little seasoning and pour the mixture over the butter.
4. Microwave the eggs on HIGH for 1 minute then lift the cooked edges from the side of the container, moving them to the middle. Continue this process, moving the eggs every 30 seconds until they are nearly cooked.
5. Allow the eggs to stand covered for 1 minute before spreading the spinach over one side of the omelette and folding the other half over it.

Welsh Rarebit   *S/L Easy*

Total cooking time: 2 mins.

It is preferable to heat the cheese mixture separately, then pour it onto freshly toasted bread. For a change, add some chopped spring onions.

Ingredients	Metric	Imperial
Cheese, grated	50g	2 oz
Brown ale	15ml sp	1 tbsp
Mustard powder	¼ x 5ml sp	¼ tsp
Butter	knob	knob
Salt and ground black pepper		
Toasted bread slice, hot	1	1

Method

1. Mix together the cheese, brown ale, mustard, butter and seasoning.
2. Microwave on MEDIUM/50% for about 2 minutes or until melted and hot. Stir once or twice during heating.
3. Pour the mixture over the hot toast and serve immediately.

Quick Egg Florentine   *S/L/M Easy*

Total cooking time: 4–5 mins.

Use a mature cheese for this recipe for the best flavour.

Ingredients	Metric	Imperial
Frozen chopped spinach, defrosted	100g	4 oz
on DEFROST/30% for 2–3 minutes (and stand for 3 minutes)		
Strong Cheddar cheese, grated	25g	1 oz
Egg, size 2 or 3	1	1
Ground black pepper		

Method

1. Place the spinach in a small shallow container, cover and cook on HIGH for 1½ minutes.

2. Sprinkle the cheese over the spinach then carefully break the egg on the top. Prick the yolk.
3. Cover and microwave on MEDIUM/50% for 2–3 minutes or until the egg is just set.
4. Season well with black pepper and serve with crusty fresh bread.

13. PASTA & RICE & PIZZAS

Pasta and rice both cook well in the microwave, particularly in small quantities. There is not a great time-saving as they take the same time to cook, no matter what the quantity. However, convenience makes it a worthwhile method. Pasta and rice reheat superbly in the microwave too. There may be occasions, when you wish to save time, when you will want to cook the pasta on the hob while a sauce is being prepared in the microwave — or vice versa. Always add boiling water to the pasta or rice. A little cooking oil in the water prevents the shapes or grains from sticking together.

Pizzas are successful in the microwave too, particularly if cooked on a browning dish. See the recipes for details.

General method for pasta
1. Place 75g/3 oz pasta shapes (or spaghetti, broken to fit the container) in a deep container.
2. Stir in $\frac{1}{2}$–1 x 5ml sp/$\frac{1}{2}$–1 tsp cooking oil and salt to taste.
3. Pour 900ml/1$\frac{1}{2}$ pt boiling water over the pasta and stir.
4. Cover and cook on HIGH for 7–10 minutes (a little longer for wholewheat pasta), or until the pasta is just slightly undercooked.

5. Allow it to stand, covered, for 3–5 minutes before draining and using.

General method for rice
1. Place 50g/2 oz long grain rice in a deep container and stir in ½–1 x 5ml sp/½–1 tsp cooking oil and salt to taste.
2. Pour over 200ml/7 fl oz boiling water and stir.
3. Cover and microwave on HIGH for 8–9 minutes. Do not stir.
4. Allow the rice to stand covered for 5–8 minutes before fluffing up with a fork and serving.

Brown rice: may need an extra 75ml/3 fl oz boiling water and an extra 10 minutes cooking time.

Cannelloni
L/M Needs a little extra care

Total cooking time: 7–8½ mins.

This recipe uses cheese and spinach to fill the cannelloni tubes. Try it with the Bolognese sauce on page 64. Use lasagne sheets to roll around the filling if you cannot get cannelloni tubes.

Ingredients	*Metric*	*Imperial*
Cannelloni tubes	3	3
Cooking oil	5ml sp	1 tsp
Frozen spinach, defrosted on DEFROST/30% for 2–3 minutes (and stand for 3 minutes), and drained	50g	2 oz
Curd or cream cheese	25g	1 oz
Mace, ground	good pinch	good pinch
Salt and ground black pepper		
Spring onions, chopped	3	3
Can of tomatoes	230g	8 oz
Butter or margarine	knob	knob
Basil, dried	½–1 x 5ml sp	½–1 tsp
Cheddar cheese, grated	25g	1 oz

Method
1. Place the cannelloni tubes and cooking oil in a deep container, cover with boiling water and microwave on HIGH for 3–4 minutes, or until they are just soft.
2. Drain the cannelloni and allow them to cool in a damp tea towel.
3. Meanwhile mix together the spinach, curd or cream cheese and mace, seasoning well.
4. Fill the cannelloni tubes with this mixture and arrange them in a shallow microwave container.
5. Put the remaining ingredients (except the Cheddar cheese) into a small microwave bowl, chopping the tomatoes into their juice. Cover and microwave on HIGH for 3 minutes.
6. Season the tomato sauce with salt and ground black pepper and pour it over the cannelloni. Sprinkle with the Cheddar cheese and microwave on HIGH uncovered for 1–1½ minutes or until the cheese melts.

Pasta with Devilled Chicken Livers

S/L/M Easy

Total cooking time: 8 mins.

This chicken liver mixture is also delicious with rice or on toast.

Ingredients	Metric	Imperial
Small pasta shapes	50g	2 oz
Vegetable oil	½–1 x 5ml sp	½–1 tsp
Water, boiling	550ml	1 pt
Sherry	5ml sp	1 tsp
Worcestershire sauce	5ml sp	1 tsp
Tabasco sauce	2 drops	2 drops
Tomato purée	2 x 5ml sp	2 tsp

Whole grain mustard	5ml sp	1 tsp
Tarragon, dried	½ x 5ml sp	½ tsp
Ground black pepper		
Chicken livers, cut into 2.5cm/1 inch pieces	100g	4 oz
Button mushrooms, sliced	50g	2 oz
Seedless grapes, halved	25g	1 oz

Method
1. Put the pasta into a deep container with the vegetable oil. Pour the boiling water over it, cover and microwave on HIGH for 5 minutes.
2. Allow the pasta to stand while you prepare the livers.
3. Mix together the sherry, Worcestershire Sauce, tabasco, tomato purée, mustard, tarragon and pepper.
4. Stir in the chicken livers, cover and microwave on MEDIUM/50% for 1½ minutes.
5. Stir in the mushrooms, cover and microwave on MEDIUM/50% for another 1½ minutes.
6. Stir in the grapes, cover and allow the dish to stand for 2 minutes.
7. Drain the pasta and stir in the devilled chicken livers and serve.

Tagliatelli with Creamy Cheese and Nut Sauce

L/M Easy

Total cooking time: 5–6 mins.

Instead of freshly crushed garlic and herbs, try using the ready-made cream cheese with garlic and herbs added. Use low fat cheese and yoghurt if you wish.

Ingredients	Metric	Imperial
Green tagliatelli	50g	2 oz
Vegetable oil	½–1 x 5ml sp	½–1 tsp
Water, boiling	550ml	1 pt
Soft cheese such as curd or quark	3 x 15ml sp	3 tbsp
Spring onion, chopped finely	1	1
Parsley, chopped	2 x 5ml sp	2 tsp
Garlic clove(s), crushed	1–2	1–2
Dried basil	2 x 5ml sp	2 tsp
Nuts, chopped, such as walnuts	15ml sp	1 tbsp
Cream or yoghurt	2 x 15ml sp	2 tbsp
Ground black pepper		

Method

1. Place the pasta and vegetable oil in a deep container and pour the boiling water over it. Cover and microwave on HIGH for 5–6 minutes or until the pasta is just cooked.
2. Mix together the remaining ingredients in a separate bowl.
3. Drain the tagliatelli, stir in the sauce and serve straightaway.

Savoury Rice   *L/M Easy*

Total cooking time: 10 mins.

Adding some cooked meat such as ham or chicken, or fish such as tuna or salmon at stage 2 makes this a very substantial meal.

Ingredients	Metric	Imperial
Long grain rice	50g	2 oz
Vegetable oil	½ x 5ml sp	½ tsp
Water, boiling	200ml	7 fl oz
Turmeric	¼ x 5ml sp	¼ tsp

Spring onions, chopped	2	2
Frozen peas	25g	1 oz
Frozen sweetcorn	25g	1 oz
Button mushrooms, sliced	25g	1 oz
Parsley, chopped	15ml sp	1 tbsp
Salt and ground black pepper		

Method
1. Place the rice and vegetable oil in a deep container and pour the boiling water over. Stir in the turmeric and microwave covered on HIGH for 7 minutes.
2. Add the onions, peas, sweetcorn and mushrooms and cover and microwave on HIGH for a further 3 minutes.
3. Stir in the parsley and seasoning to taste, cover and allow the rice to stand for 3 minutes before serving.

Pizza-Topped Crumpets   *S/L/M Easy*

Total cooking time: 2–2½ mins.

A deliciously-quick pizza-type snack without the time-consuming method!

Ingredients	*Metric*	*Imperial*
Bacon rashers	2	2
Butter or margarine	knob	knob
Crumpets	2	2
Tomato, sliced	1	1
Mixed herbs	¼ x 5ml sp	¼ tsp
Salt and ground black pepper		
Cheese, grated	2 x 15ml sp	2 tbsp

Method
1. Place the bacon rashers on a microwave rack on a plate and cover with a sheet of kitchen paper. Microwave on HIGH for 1 minute.
2. Spread a little butter on each crumpet and place them on a plate.

3. Arrange the tomato slices on the crumpets and chop the bacon over them.
4. Sprinkle over the herbs and seasoning to taste.
5. Top with the grated cheese and microwave on HIGH for 1–1½ minutes or until the cheese has melted.

Personalised Pizzas

S/L Easy

Total cooking time: 3 mins.

Keep packs of individual cheese and tomato pizzas in the freezer. Add toppings to suit yourself — to make a snack or substantial meal with a mixed salad. A browning dish gives best results.

Topping suggestions:
Chopped green pepper and mushrooms
Anchovies and black olives
Lashings of fresh (or dried) herbs and extra cheese
Crispy bacon and sweetcorn kernels
Ham and mushrooms

Method
1. Pre-heat browning dish on HIGH for about 4 minutes (check with the manufacturer's instructions).
2. Add ½–1 x 15ml sp/½–1 tbsp cooking oil then the frozen pizza with its topping.
3. Microwave on HIGH for about 3 minutes or until the cheese in the centre of the pizza bubbles.
4. Allow the pizza to stand on the browning dish for 2–3 minutes before serving.

Fresh Wholewheat Pizza   *L/M Easy*

Total cooking time: 5½–7 mins.

It would be worth doubling the quantity and freezing one
pizza for defrosting and reheating on another occasion.

Ingredients	Metric	Imperial
Base:		
Wholewheat self-raising flour	100g	4 oz
Baking powder	½ x 5ml sp	½ tsp
Mustard powder	¼ x 5ml sp	¼ tsp
Salt	pinch	pinch
Ground black pepper	pinch	pinch
Butter or margarine	20g	¾ oz
Egg, size 3, beaten	½	½
Milk	3 x 15ml sp	3 tbsp
Topping:		
Spring onions, chopped	3	3
Mushrooms, sliced	50g	2 oz
Tomato, sliced	1	1
Ham, chopped	small slice	small slice
Dried mixed herbs	½ x 5ml sp	½ tsp
Cheese, grated	50g	2 oz

Method
Base:
1. Mix the flour, baking powder, mustard powder, salt and
   black pepper, then rub in the butter until the mixture
   resembles fine breadcrumbs.
2. Stir in the beaten egg and milk and mix it into a soft
   dough.
3. Roll out the dough on a lightly floured surface into a
   20cm/8 in circle.
4. Place the dough circle on a plate lined with non-stick or
   greaseproof paper.
5. Microwave on HIGH for 1½–2 minutes or until the dough
   is risen and just dry on its surface.

6. Allow the pizza base to stand for 2–3 minutes before lifting it off the greaseproof paper.
7. Wipe the plate of any moisture and carefully replace the pizza without the greaseproof paper.

Topping:
8. Arrange the topping ingredients over the pizza base, finishing with the grated cheese.
9. Microwave uncovered on HIGH for 4–5 minutes or until the cheese in the centre of the pizza is bubbling.
10. Allow the pizza to stand for 3 minutes before serving.

14. DESSERTS

With the microwave you can prepare individual puddings speedily and at little extra expense. Sponge and suet puddings, and Christmas puddings, which would normally need hours of steaming conventionally, cook in minutes. Fruits cooked in the microwave are tender and remain beautifully whole. Remember to split the skin of whole fruit such as apples, and cut other fruits into equal-sized pieces to encourage even cooking.

Oranges in Caramel
L/M Easy

Total cooking time: 3½–5 mins.

A fresh fruit can be transformed with the help of the microwave.

Ingredients	Metric	Imperial
Orange juice	3 x 15ml sp	3 tbsp
Rum (optional)	5ml sp	1 tsp
Sultanas	½ x 15ml sp	½ tbsp
Caster sugar	25g	1 oz
Water	3 x 15ml sp	3 tbsp
Orange, seedless, if possible	1	1

Method

1. Put the orange juice, rum (optional) and sultanas into a small microwave container. Cover and microwave on HIGH for 1 minute.
2. Put the sugar and water into another bowl and microwave on HIGH for 1 minute. Stir well to dissolve the sugar completely.
3. Microwave the sugar mixture again on HIGH, stirring every 30 seconds, until the syrup turns a pale golden brown.
4. Allow the syrup to cool for a few minutes before slowly adding the orange juice. Microwave on HIGH for 30 seconds.
5. Peel the orange, removing the pith and any seeds. Slice and pour the syrup over the orange.
6. Serve hot or chilled.

Banana – Tropical Style   *S/L/M Easy*

Total cooking time: 1–1½ mins.

Use a firm banana so that it keeps its shape.

Ingredients	Metric	Imperial
Banana, peeled, sliced thickly	1	1
Lemon or lime juice	5ml sp	1 tsp
Orange, segmented	1 small	1 small

Butter or margarine	knob	knob
Demerara sugar	1–2 x 5ml sp	1–2 tsp
Desiccated coconut	2 x 5ml sp	2 tsp
Raisins	15ml sp	1 tbsp
Pineapple juice	15ml sp	1 tbsp

Method
1. Toss the banana slices in lemon or lime juice and mix them with the orange segments.
2. Add the butter or margarine. Mix together the remaining ingredients and add these too.
3. Cover and microwave on HIGH for 1–1½ minutes. Serve while hot.

Queen of Puddings   *L/M Easy*

Total cooking time: 2–2½ mins.

This traditional pudding will not have a crisp finish. Sprinkle the meringue with chopped nuts to add crunch.

Ingredients	*Metric*	*Imperial*
Egg, size 4 or 5, separated	1	1
Demerara sugar	5ml sp	1 tsp
Butter or margarine	knob	knob
Milk	75ml	3 fl oz
Lemon rind, grated	½ x 5ml sp	½ tsp
Breadcrumbs, fresh	5 x 15ml sp	5 tbsp
Frozen raspberries, blackberries, gooseberries or plums	2 x 15ml sp	2 tbsp
Caster sugar	15ml sp	1 tbsp
Walnuts or hazelnuts, chopped	½ x 15ml sp	½ tbsp

Method
1. Mix together the egg yolk, demerara sugar, butter and milk, and microwave uncovered on HIGH for 30 seconds.
2. Stir in the lemon rind and the breadcrumbs and spoon the mixture into a small dish.
3. Sprinkle the frozen fruit over the breadcrumb mix.
4. Whisk the egg white until stiff, then whisk in the caster sugar to make the meringue.
5. Spoon the meringue over the fruit, sprinkle it with chopped nuts and microwave uncovered on HIGH for 1½–2 minutes.

Sponge Pudding with Jam Sauce　　　*L/M Easy*

Total cooking time: 2½–3 mins.

A mini version of everyone's favourite home-made pud!

Ingredients	*Metric*	*Imperial*
Self-raising flour	40g	1½ oz
Soft margarine	25g	1 oz
Caster sugar	25g	1 oz
Egg, size 5, beaten	1	1
Vanilla flavouring	few drops	few drops
Milk	2 x 5ml sp	2 tsp
Jam	2 x 15ml sp	2 tbsp
Water	2 x 5ml sp	2 tsp
Lemon or orange juice	few drops	few drops

Method
1. Beat together the flour, margarine, sugar, egg, vanilla flavouring and milk until smooth.
2. Put the mixture into a small bowl or teacup (lightly greased) and smooth the top.
3. Cover loosely and microwave on HIGH for 1½–2 minutes.
4. Remove the cover and allow the pudding to stand for 2 minutes before turning it out.

5. Meanwhile microwave the remaining ingredients in a small bowl or jug, on HIGH for 1 minute.
6. Stir the jam sauce well and pour it over the pudding.

Cinnamon Apple Crumble   *L/M Easy*

Total cooking time: 1–1¼ mins.

A deliciously quick pudding — serve with cream or custard flavoured with a little cinnamon.

Ingredients	Metric	Imperial
Eating apple, sliced	1	1
Sultanas	2 x 5ml sp	2 tsp
Demerara sugar	15ml sp	1 tbsp
Cinnamon, ground	pinch	pinch
Crunchy biscuits, such as ginger or lemon cookies	2	2

Method
1. Arrange the apple in the base of a small dish and sprinkle the sultanas over.
2. Mix half the sugar with the cinnamon and sprinkle this over the apple.
3. Crush the biscuits and mix them with the remaining sugar. Sprinkle this over the apple.
4. Microwave uncovered on HIGH for 1–1¼ minutes.

Pavlova For One   *L/M Easy*

Total cooking time: 1–1¼ mins.

The proportion of sugar in this recipe is high enough to make this a once-in-a-while treat only. The conventional meringue mixture does not cook well in the microwave.

Ingredients	*Metric*	*Imperial*
Egg white	2 x 5ml sp	2 tsp
Icing sugar, sieved well	about 25g	about 1 oz
Double cream	2 x 15ml sp	2 tbsp
Fresh fruit such as halved black grapes and raspberries	3 x 15ml sp	3 tbsp
Plain chocolate	2 squares	2 squares

Method

1. Break up the egg white with a fork.
2. Use a wooden or plastic spoon to mix in the icing sugar, a little at a time, until you have a fondant-like paste which is thick enough to shape with your hands.
3. Divide the mixture into two pieces and flatten them into ½ cm/¼ inch thick circles.
4. Place the circles on a large sheet of non-stick baking paper, leaving space between the two.
5. Microwave on HIGH for about 1–1¼ minutes or until the meringue does not fall when the microwaves are switched off. If they do fall, simply switch the oven on again for a further few seconds. Take care not to overcook or the meringue will turn brown during its standing period (actually a light caramel colour produces a beautiful flavour).
6. Let the meringues cool for a few minutes before lifting them off the paper.
7. Whip the cream, spread it over one meringue, sprinkle the fruit over and top with the second meringue.
8. In a small container microwave the chocolate on HIGH for 15 seconds or until it is melted. Use a teaspoon to dribble the chocolate over the top meringue.

Spotted Dick   *L/M Easy*

Total cooking time: 3 mins.

Use the all-in-one method of mixing to make this traditional pud in minutes. Softening the fruit first as in stage 1 below gives the best results.

Ingredients	Metric	Imperial
Water	5ml	1 tsp
Currants	25g	1 oz
Soft margarine	25g	1 oz
Caster sugar	25g	1 oz
Self-raising flour	25g	1 oz
Egg, size 5, beaten	1	1
Vanilla essence	few drops	few drops

Method
1. Place the water and currants in a small container, cover and microwave on HIGH for about 30–45 seconds. This plumps up and softens the fruit.
2. Beat together the remaining ingredients until thoroughly mixed.
3. Lightly grease a cup or small pudding basin.
4. Fold the currants and liquid into the cake mixture and turn it into the prepared cup or basin.
5. Microwave uncovered for 2–2½ minutes.
6. Allow the pudding to stand for 2 minutes before turning it out.

Orange Chocolate Pots

L/M Easy

Total cooking time: 3–4 mins.

Always use the microwave to melt chocolate for a recipe. It is much simpler than the usual method using a bowl over a pan of boiling water.

Ingredients	Metric	Imperial
Orange chocolate cake covering	50g	2 oz
Egg, size 3, separated	1	1
Double or whipping cream, whipped	30ml	2 tbsp

Method
1. Microwave the chocolate pieces in a bowl on MEDIUM/50% for about 3–4 minutes, stirring once or twice, or until the chocolate has melted.
2. Allow the chocolate to cool slightly, then beat in the egg yolk until the mixture is glossy and smooth.
3. Stir in the whipped cream.
4. Whisk the egg white until it forms stiff peaks then fold it gently into the chocolate mix.
5. Turn the mixture into a glass or serving dish and chill for about 1 hour before serving.

Baked Egg Custard   *L/M Easy*

Total cooking time: 6–7 mins.

A single baked egg custard is ready to eat in just 15 minutes!

Ingredients	*Metric*	*Imperial*
Milk	150ml	¼ pt
Egg, size 3, lightly beaten	1	1
Caster sugar	1–2 x 5ml sp	1–2 tsp
Vanilla essence	drop	drop
Nutmeg, grated		

Method
1. In a small jug, microwave the milk on HIGH for 1 minute.
2. Mix together the egg, sugar and vanilla essence and lightly whisk in the warmed milk.
3. Strain the mixture into a straight-sided container and sprinkle some grated nutmeg over it.
4. Microwave uncovered on MEDIUM/50% for 5–6 minutes or until just set.
5. Allow the custard to stand for 5 minutes before serving.

Pear with Melba Sauce   *L/M Easy*

Total cooking time: 4–5 mins.

Treat yourself to this glamorous pud. The sauce can be served hot or cold.

Ingredients	Metric	Imperial
Pear, whole, peeled	1 large	1 large
Apple juice or water	60ml	4 tbsp
Caster sugar	2 x 5ml sp	2 tsp
Cornflour	½ x 5ml sp	½ tsp
Raspberries, fresh or frozen, defrosted on DEFROST/30% for 2 minutes (and stand for 3 minutes), puréed or sieved	75g	3 oz
Lemon juice	½ x 5ml sp	½ tsp

Method
1. Place the pear in a shallow dish with the apple juice or water, cover and microwave on HIGH for 3 minutes or until the pear is just tender. Allow it to stand covered while the sauce is prepared.
2. In another small bowl or jug, mix together the sugar and cornflour with 10ml/2 tsp water.
3. Stir in the raspberry purée and microwave uncovered on HIGH for 1–2 minutes, stirring every 30 seconds, or until the sauce is thick.
4. Stir the lemon juice into the sauce.
5. Drain and discard the liquid from the pear (or you could add it to the Melba Sauce to make a very thin pouring consistency). Pour the sauce over the pear and serve.

Sweet White Sauce   *S/L/M Easy*

Total cooking time: 2½–3 mins.

Serve this with sponge and fruit puddings. Stir in a little single cream after stage 4 for special occasions.

Ingredients	Metric	Imperial
Butter	15g	½ oz
Flour	15g	½ oz
Milk	150ml	¼ pt
Caster sugar	½–1 x 15ml sp	½–1 tbsp

Method

1. In a small bowl or jug, microwave the butter on HIGH for 30 seconds or until melted.
2. Stir in the flour and gradually blend in the milk.
3. Microwave, uncovered, on HIGH for 2–3 minutes, stirring every 30 seconds, until the sauce is boiling and rising up the sides of the container.
4. Stir in the sugar and allow the sauce to stand for 2 minutes.

Brandy Sauce: Add 5ml/1 tsp brandy after stage 4.
Chocolate Sauce: Stir in 15ml sp/1 tbsp grated chocolate with the sugar at stage 3.
Spicy Sauce: Add ¼ x 5ml sp/¼ tsp mixed spice during stage 2.

INDEX

Words and numbers in italics refer to actual recipes.

A

Adjusting cooking times, 28, 29
Advance programming, 15, 16
Advantages of microwave cooking, 11 *et seq.*
Apple Crumble, Cinnamon, 115
Artichokes, 82
Asparagus, 82
Aubergines, 82
Automatic sensor, 17

B

Bacon and Olive Kebabs, 41
   chop, 63
   Hash, 72–3
   rashers, 62
   , Somerset, 72
   —Topped Potato, 71
Baked Egg Custard, 118
   Vegetables, 90
Banana – Tropical Style, 112–13
Baskets, 18
Batter-coated foods, 12
Beans, 83
Beansprouts, 83
Beef Kebabs with Herbs, 65
Beefburgers, 63
Beetroot, 83
Blind people, 17

Bobouti, 66–7
Boil-in-the-bags, 20, 49, 82
Boiled egg, 12, 95
Boiling water, 12
Bolognese Sauce, 64–5
Bowls, 19, 21
Braille panels, 17
Bread, crusty, 12
   Roll, 33
   , 'Crostini', 46–7
Breakfasts, 32 *et seq.*
Broccoli, 83
   , *Cheesy, 88–9*
Browning dish, 20, 61
   element, 16, 61
   food, 61, 62
   powders, 61
Brussels sprouts, 83
Butter and Mustard Sauce, Trout with, 54
   , adding, 50
Buttered Plaice with Capers, 56–7

C

Cabbage, 83
   , *Gingered, 89–90*
   with Ham and Yoghurt, 93–4
Calorie intake, 25
Cannelloni, 103–4
Cardboard, 18

Cardiac pacemakers, 10
Carrots, 83
Casserole, Vegetable, 87
Casseroles, 21, 27
Cauliflower, 83
Celery, 83
Ceramic, 19
Cheese Sauce, 47–8
 – Topped Baked Eggs, 95–6
Cheeseburger, 68–9
Cheesy Broccoli, 88–9
Chicken breasts, 63, 64
    Curry, 73–4
    drumsticks, 63
    , Spicy, 74
    in Red Wine, 75
    joint, 63
Chilli, 65–6
Choosing a microwave oven,
    14 *et seq.*
Chops, 62, 63
Cinnamon Apple Crumble, 115
Cling film, 20
Cod and Lime Kebabs, 50–1
Coffee, 32
Colour of ovens, 17
Combination ovens, 16
Containers, 18 *et seq.*, 27
Conversion tables, 30, 31
Cooking smells, 13
    times, 28, 29
    , fish, 50
    , meat, 63
    , vegetables, 82–3
Corn on the cob, 83
    with Garlic Butter, 91
Cost, 11, 15
Cottage Pie, Spicy, 67–8
*Courgette and Carrot Soup
    with Tagliatelli,* 45–6
Courgettes, 83
    , Greek-Style, 84
Covering food, 27, 49, 62, 82

Croissants, 33
'Crostini' Bread Roll, 46–7
Croûtons, Herb, 42–3
Crumpets, Pizza-Topped, 107–8
Crusty bread, 12
Cucumber Sauce, Salmon with,
    51–2
Curry, Chicken, 73–4

D
Deep-fat frying, 12
Defrosting food, 26, 82
Desserts, 111 et seq.
Disabled people, 12, 17
Doors, oven, 15
Duck, 63
    with Fruity Sauce, 79–80

E
Egg and Leek Pot, 96–7
    , boiled, 12, 95
    Custard, Baked, 118
    Florentine, Quick, 100–1
    , Poached, 33
Eggs, Cheese-Topped Baked,
    95–6
    in their shells, 12, 95
    with Herb and Garlic Cheese,
    Scrambled, 97
    Mushroom and Cheese,
    Scrambled, 98
Elderly people, 12, 17
Energy, 11
Equipment, 18 et seq.

F
Fat, adding, 26
    intake, 25
Fibre, 25
Fish, 49 et seq.
    cooking times, 50
    with a Spanish Flavour, 52–3
Foil, 18, 49, 61

Freezer, 22, 23
French Onion Soup, 42–3
Fruit, 111

G
Gammon steak, 63
Gingered Cabbage, 89–90
Glass, 19
  ceramic, 18
Grill, 16, 23, 61, 62

H
Haddock 'Crumble', Smoked, 53–4
Ham and Egg in Wholemeal Roll, 34–5
Healthy eating, 24 *et seq.*
Herb Croûtons, 42–3
Hob, 23
Honeyed Lamb with Rosemary, 78
  Spare Ribs, 69–70

I
Ingredients at room temperature, 22, 30

J
Jugs, 21

K
Kebabs, Bacon and Olive, 41
  , Cod and Lime, 50–1
  with Herbs, Beef, 65
Kedgeree, Smoky, 36
Kippers with Tartare Sauce, 57–8
Kitchen paper, 18, 21, 62

L
Lamb chop, 63
  Skewers, Minty, 77–8
  with Rosemary, Honeyed, 78

Lean Meat Pâté, 37–8
Leeks, 83
Lemony Liver, 77
Lentil Soup, 44
Liver, 63
  , Lemony, 77
  Stir-Fry, 76
Low-fat cooking, 12

M
Magnetron, 15
Marrow, 83
Meat, 61 *et seq.*
Metal containers, 18
Microwave oven bags, 19, 49, 61, 82
  rack, 21, 62
Milk, 33
Mince, 62, 63
Minty Lamb Skewers, 77–8
Moules Marinière, 59–60
Mousse, Sweetcorn, 38–9
Moving microwave ovens, 12, 15
Mushroom Sauce, 48
Mushrooms, 83
  à la Greque, 84–5
Mustard Sauce, Trout with Butter and, 54

N
NACNE Report, 24, 25
Nutrition, 12, 25 *et seq.*

O
Omelette, Spinach-Filled, 98–9
Onion Sauce, 47–8
  Soup, French, 42–3
  with Stilton and Walnuts, 88
Onions, 83
Orange Chocolate Pots, 117–8
Oranges in Caramel, 111–12
Oven-cleaning, 13

Ovenglass, 18

P
Pancakes, 12
Paper, 18
Parsley Sauce, 47–8
Parsnips, 83
Pasta, 102–3
   *with Devilled Chicken Livers,
   104–5*
Pastry, 16
Pâté, Lean Meat, 37–8
Pavlova For One, 115–6
Pea Soup, Quick, 40–1
Pear with Melba Sauce, 119
Peas, 83
Pepper with Cheese, 86
Personalised Pizzas, 108
Pies, 12
*Pizza, Fresh Wholewheat,
   109–10*
   – Topped Crumpets, 107–8
Pizzas, 102
   , Personalised, 108
*Plaice with Capers, Buttered,
   56–7*
Plastic, 18, 19
   bags, 19
Poached Egg, 33
'Polyunsaturated' fats, 25
Poppadums, 48
Pork chop, 63
   *with Apple and Walnut
   Stuffing, 70–1*
Porridge, 34
Potato, Bacon-Topped, 71
   *, Spinach and Cheese
   Stuffed, 92–3*
   , Tasty Layered, 85–6
Potatoes, 83
Pottery, 18
Poultry, 61 *et seq.*
Prawn Sauce, 47–8

Prawns in Tomato Sauce, 55
   , Sweet and Sour, 58–9
*Prune and Grapefruit Compote,
   35*
Puddings, 110 *et seq.*

Q
Quantities for one, 50, 63,
   82–3
Queen of Puddings, 113–4
Quick Egg Florentine, 100–1
   Pea Soup, 40–1

R
Refrigerator, 22
Reheating food, 26, 102
Rice, 102–3
   , Savoury, 106–7
Ring shape containers, 19
Roast dishes, 16
Roasting bags, 19, 49, 61, 82

S
*Salmon with Cucumber Sauce,
   51–2*
Salt, adding, 26, 50, 62, 82
   intake, 25
'Saturated' fats, 25
Sauces, 47–8, 51–2, 54, 55,
   64–5, 119–20
Sausages, 63
Savoury Rice, 106–7
*Scrambled Eggs with Herb and
   Garlic Cheese, 97*
   Mushroom and Cheese, 98
Sizes of microwave ovens, 12,
   14, 15, 16
*Smoked Haddock 'Crumble',
   53–4*
Smoky Kedgeree, 36
Somerset Bacon, 72
Soups, 27, 39 *et seq.*
Spare Ribs, Honeyed, 69–70

Speed of cooking, 11
Spicy Chicken Drumsticks, 74
    Cottage Pie, 67–8
Spinach, 83
    and Cheese Stuffed Potato,
    92–3
    – Filled Omelette, 98–9
*Sponge Pudding with Jam
    Sauce*, 114–115
Spoon measures, 31
Spotted Dick, 116–7
Standing times, 30
Starters, 37 *et seq.*
Steak, 63
Steam, 13, 20
Stir-Fry Liver, 76
    with Tuna, 55–6
Stirring food, 27, 82
Stock Pot, 41–2
Stoneware, 18
Stuffed Tomato, 91–2
Sugar intake, 25
Swedes, 83
Sweet and Sour Prawns, 58–9
    White Sauce, 119–20
*Sweetcorn and Crispy Bacon
    Soup*, 39–40
    Mousse, 38–9
Symbols, 30

T
*Tagliatelli with Creamy Cheese
    and Nut Sauce*, 105–6

Tandoori Turkey, 79
Tasty Layered Potato, 85–6
Tea, 33
Thick Vegetable Soup, 44–5
Toast, 12
Tomato Sauce, Prawns in, 55
    , Stuffed, 91–2
Tomatoes, 83
*Trout with Butter and Mustard
    Sauce*, 54
Tuna, Stir-Fry with, 55–6
Turkey, Tandoori, 79
Turning food, 27, 62
Turnips 83

V
Variable control, 15, 29
Vegetable Casserole, 87
    Soup, Thick, 44–5
Vegetables, 81 *et seq.*
    , Baked, 90
Ventilation, 14

W
Washing-up, 13
Water, boiling, 12
Wattages, 15, 16, 28
Waxed paper, 18
Welsh Rarebit, 99–100
White Sauce, 47–8
    , Sweet, 119–20
Wood, 18

OUR PUBLISHING POLICY

HOW WE CHOOSE

Our policy is to consider deserving manuscripts and we can give special editorial help where an author is an authority on his subject but an inexperienced writer. We are rigorously selective in the choice of books we publish. We set the highest standards of editorial quality and accuracy. This means that a *Paperfront* is easy to understand and delightful to read. Where illustrations are necessary to convey points of detail, these are drawn up by a subject specialist artist from our panel.

HOW WE KEEP PRICES LOW

We aim for the big seller. This enables us to order enormous print runs and achieve the lowest price for you. Unfortunately, this means that you will not find in the *Paperfront* list any titles on obscure subjects of minority interest only. These could not be printed in large enough quantities to be sold for the low price at which we offer this series. We sell almost all our *Paperfronts* at the same unit price. This saves a lot of fiddling about in our clerical departments and helps us to give you world-beating value. Under this system, the longer titles are offered at a price which we believe to be unmatched by any publisher in the world.

OUR DISTRIBUTION SYSTEM

Because of the competitive price, and the rapid turnover, *Paperfronts* are possibly the most profitable line a bookseller can handle. They are stocked by the best bookshops all over the world. It may be that your bookseller has run out of stock of a particular title. If so, he can order more from us at any time—we have a fine reputation for 'same day' despatch, and we supply any order, however small (even a single copy), to any bookseller who has an account with us. We prefer you to buy from your bookseller, as this reminds him of the strong underlying public demand for *Paperfronts*. Members of the public who live in remote places, or who are housebound, or whose local bookseller is unco-operative, can order direct from us by post.

FREE

If you would like an up-to-date list of all paperfront titles currently available, send a stamped self-addressed envelope to
ELLIOT RIGHT WAY BOOKS, BRIGHTON RD.,
LOWER KINGSWOOD, SURREY, U.K.